WHAT'S YOUR BIAS?

WHAT'S YOUR BIAS?

THE SURPRISING SCIENCE OF WHY WE VOTE THE WAY WE DO

LEE DE-WIT

First published 2017 by
Elliott and Thompson Limited
27 John Street, London WC1N 2BX
www.eandtbooks.com

ISBN: 978-1-78396-350-8

9 8 7 6 5 4 3 2 1

A catalogue record for this book is available from the British Library.

Typesetting: Marie Doherty
Printed in the UK by TJ International Ltd.

CONTENTS

INTRODUCTION:
THE POLITICAL ANIMAL

Political certainties are like the Berlin Wall. They appear to be concrete and immoveable, but they can crumble and fall almost overnight. In the last two years we have seen a particularly noticeable accumulation of such rubble, with political pundits as surprised as the rest of us by event after unforeseen event.

Donald Trump wasn't expected to win the Republican nomination, let alone become president; UKIP was meant to be a sideshow in the UK, and Nigel Farage just the drunk uncle of British politics; and the polls promised Theresa May a thumping majority in the 2017 election, not a net loss of twelve seats.

So what do all of these confounding results tell us?

Well, firstly, it seems to be increasingly difficult to predict how people are going to vote. And secondly, we are witnessing the emergence of huge, and sometimes painful, political schisms.

Delve into this a little further, and it looks like many traditional political loyalties are starting to break down. Class is increasingly less important as a predictor of voting in the UK, and the customary labels of left and right wing are becoming less clearly defined.

A range of curious correlations are also emerging between the way people vote and their psychological profile. In the EU referendum, for example, although class and education level were clearly correlated with how people voted, there was also a surprising link with views on capital punishment: according to Stian Westlake, head of research at the think tank Nesta, class status and income yielded 55 per cent accuracy as to voter intention (that's significant, but not all that significant when you consider that a guess would give you 50 per cent). However, the answers to questions such as, 'Do you think criminals should be publicly whipped?' or 'Are you in favour of the death penalty?' yielded over 70 per cent accuracy for an 'out' vote.

Is this simply coincidence? Or is there something about the psychology of voters that creates this connection?

In this book, I want to examine these kinds of correlations from a different angle. I want to get under the skin of our political decision-making to try to discover whether there are meaningful psychological differences that predict – and influence – how we vote.

I'm not intending to offer an academic overview of political psychology; my primary focus is on the politics and trends of Western democracies; and I'm not going to concentrate on many of the demographic factors (like age, class and education) traditionally identified in political science as important predictors of how we vote. Rather I'm going to try to bring the psychology of politics to life, by selecting some of the key studies and setting them in the context of contemporary politics.

The science underpinning the book can offer some genuine surprises. You probably take for granted, for example, that (on average) people are likely to vote in a similar way to their parents. That is correct, but you might be surprised to learn that a large part of the reason is not down to upbringing but because of genetic similarities. In fact, the link between our political attitudes and our genetics is probably one of the most robust findings in political psychology – replicated in numerous studies since it was first demonstrated in the 1970s.

I've said that people find this link surprising, but what's stranger still is that you might be *more* surprised if you're left wing; research suggests that people on the right are more likely to think that genes or biology affect human behaviour.

This doesn't mean, however, that our political attitudes are dictated by our genes; the way we look at the world and make decisions is shaped by many different factors. While we now know that genes influence the probability of holding certain political views (and even the likelihood of voting), we still don't know which genes are responsible for this. And we certainly don't know how they might cause complex behaviours. It is unlikely that genes directly determine our political beliefs; rather, our genetic make-up results in subtle physiological or neural differences that influence our world view, personality and, ultimately, our political opinions.

Over the course of this book we will see that political opinions and psychological biases are associated in ways that we (both voters and researchers) often find surprising. Again, the fact that we are so taken aback is significant; it shows that we are not aware of some of the reasons why we vote the way we do. But the truth is that these 'implicit' or 'unconscious' biases have an effect on many of the ways we behave.

Sometimes biases involve obviously prejudicial thoughts towards a certain group that may cause us to respond incorrectly or irrationally in some way. Indeed, sometimes a bias can clearly be defined as something that deviates from what is objectively correct, where our perception and beliefs simply don't match the facts. However, in many cases defining what is sensible or correct and what is irrational is far from straightforward (and may in fact be philosophically impossible for some issues).

Race and gender are two examples where unfortunately people still experience prejudice; however, these are also particularly complex topics that affect many aspects of our society beyond the scope of politics. Most of us are, at least in principle, aware of the difficulties posed by racism and sexism in society, and, as they are addressed in great detail in other books and articles, they are not tackled in this book. That might seem an odd exclusion, but I have tried to concentrate more on the biases and psychological influences that are less well known.

Many of the biases in this book reflect subtle intuitive responses that we make so effortlessly that we don't notice them at all. Sometimes our biases only become clear when we realise that not everyone responds in the same way. And, as we will see, that can help us understand why some people make different political choices.

Let's take the issues of nationalism and immigration, one of the areas in which there has perhaps been the most left–right polarisation in recent years. Political ideology (and, unfortunately, racism) plays a role here, but over the course of the book, I'll hopefully be able to show that there are also subtle – and surprising – differences in our moral intuitions that might colour our view of nationalism. We'll take a look, for example, at the work of American social psychologist Jonathan Haidt, who has shown that responses to moral questions such as whether you would publicly bet against your favourite sports team, or whether you consider group loyalty more important than individual interests, can actually indicate whether you identify as left or right wing, and can be a good predictor of how people vote. And in turn, I think, that can help us to understand why nationalism is such a divisive issue.

These are the sorts of ideas we will explore in this book, looking at the many factors that shape the 'political animal': our world view, personality and the way we vote, and why they can make it so difficult to understand other points of view.

We'll see how ideas about fairness affect our attitude to taxation and benefits; how the different ways we perceive and respond to threats can shape our attitude to immigration; how a person's appearance can cause us to make snap judgements on their competence; how we seek information that confirms our existing outlook and reject that which challenges it.

We will see how the traditional labels of 'left wing' and 'right wing' can still be useful for understanding our changing political environment. We will also be asking what role the media plays in manipulating our political attitudes, what challenges are presented by the rise in fake news and misinformation, and what dangers arise when companies and campaigns target potential voters using psychological profiling. Lastly, we'll consider the vital question of low voter turnout and what can be done to encourage people to actually cast their vote – for whomever they choose.

In the current political climate, a book on psychological biases could be interpreted as a manifesto against democracy (if we are so hopelessly biased, what's the point in giving us all a say in government?). However, I believe that we can all benefit from an understanding of the science of voting. For starters, it can help us recognise some of our own biases and take that recognition into account when making our decisions. And secondly, it can help us spot the way that political campaigns try to exploit our biases.

But, most of all, I hope that this book will lead to a change in the way we talk about politics. I hope that it will inspire you to have some (perhaps surprisingly) constructive and interesting conversations with people you disagree with, whether it's your right-wing uncle who keeps focusing on threats you think are exaggerated, or your left-wing cousin whose political solutions you find naive. I don't expect you'll stop disagreeing, but, armed with some of the fresh perspectives contained in this book, perhaps you'll have a clearer understanding of what it is that you are actually disagreeing about and why it's so difficult for you to see eye to eye.

And if we can all do that, we might be able to bridge some of the yawning political schisms that have opened up so dramatically in recent years.

1

IT'S NOT FAIR!

In March 2017 Republican congressman John Shimkus objected to his party's revised healthcare plan on the grounds that it was unfair to men. His argument was that by keeping the 'essential health benefits' (including maternity cover) guaranteed by the Affordable Care Act, the plan unfairly forced men to purchase prenatal coverage. It was a position that sparked widespread criticism from those who believed that the previous exclusion of maternity coverage from insurance plans had been unfair to all women, who were forced to either buy specific, more expensive coverage, or go without. Many on this side of the argument, including insurance expert and columnist Nancy Metcalf, suggested that women should be able to say, 'Fine, but in that case why should we have to pay for your Viagra or prostate cancer tests?'

Questions of fairness can be complicated and emotive. Is it fair that some people's taxes pay for other people's benefits? Is it fair that the average FTSE 100 boss is paid 150 times more than the average worker? Is it fair that taxes from long-term residents of a country pay for the healthcare of new arrivals? I suspect at least one of these questions will have raised your blood pressure a little.

From a very early age, we are highly attuned to questions of fairness – as anyone who has ever told a child they have to go to bed before an older sibling will attest. In fact studies have shown that even infants as young as two years old are sensitive to perceived unfairness.[1]

Why is this relevant to a book about political bias? Because ultimately many political arguments come down to the morality of fairness. Our moral values shape our political views and therefore influence how we vote.

In this chapter I'll outline some intriguing findings about fairness, morality and politics, and show how we often interpret things differently based on intuitions we might not even be consciously aware of.

x

We tend to think we make moral decisions as part of a considered, rational process in which we weigh up reasons for why something might be right or wrong, but frequently we can't actually explain why we have certain moral intuitions.

To demonstrate this problem, psychologists have developed a process called 'moral dumbfounding'.[2] In these experiments people are asked provocative ethical questions, such as whether it is wrong for adult siblings to have sex. Most people will certainly say yes. But things get interesting when we start to explore the reasons behind their response. Take a moment to get a sense of your own position on this particular question; why do you think it is right or wrong?

One of the most frequent explanations offered is that a child born from a brother and sister would be more likely to have a genetic defect. So let's exclude that option by stating that they use completely effective contraception, which means there is no way the sister will become pregnant.

Do you still think it would be morally wrong? Probably yes. Another common reason people give is simply that it could be terrible for their reputation if other people know they have had sex. But what if they do it just once, secretly, in a way that guarantees no one will ever find out?

When psychologists run this kind of experiment, they systematically take away all the practical reasons people might give for why this might be wrong – but the vast majority of participants remain convinced that their first reaction is correct, even though they cannot offer a justification for it. Sometimes our gut feelings about right and wrong are not actually shaped by reasoning, but the other way round: we attempt to rationalise our responses by looking for arguments to support them.

It can be hard to talk politics with people we disagree with. If you struggle to understand why people on the left are so focused on supporting the welfare state, or why people on the right are so focused on reducing taxes, you might simply have made assumptions about fairness that are completely different from theirs.

$$\boxed{X}$$

When it comes to voting, it's easy to assume that people just support the tax and welfare policies that directly benefit them. There is some truth to that, but we don't always vote in our own economic self-interest. Poor working-class voters will sometimes vote for parties that intend to reduce welfare programmes, and well-off voters will sometimes vote for higher taxes to support welfare programmes they are unlikely to use.

Psychologists have argued that to understand why people make moral decisions that don't obviously seem self-serving, we have to look at how we have evolved as a species. It might sound strange that evolution has played a role in shaping something as complicated as our moral intuitions, but there are some reasons to consider the idea.

Evolution is, by definition, a process whereby genes can only survive if the biological organism successfully reproduces. Genes, as Richard Dawkins argues, are therefore literally 'selfish': their continued existence hangs on them making it into the next generation of offspring.

In complex social organisms like humans, the ability to survive and reproduce has clearly become dependent on our ability to cooperate with other humans: sometimes we need to help others because sometimes others can help us.

And if social animals are going to cooperate, they need to develop a keen sense of fairness – to prevent individuals taking advantage of others in the group.

Other social species also seem to have developed a keen sense of fairness. In a simple but powerful experiment, Sarah Brosnan and Frans de Waal trained pairs of monkeys to perform a straightforward task for a small reward,[3] such as a grape or piece of celery. Everything worked smoothly so long as both monkeys received the same reward. But when one monkey was rewarded with celery and saw that the other monkey was being given grapes, he immediately spotted the disparity and protested about it. When it continued, he refused to eat the celery (which had previously been perfectly acceptable as a motivational reward) and threw it back in the tester's face! If you watch the videos of these experiments, you get a very vivid sense of the monkey's visceral emotional response, which most of us can probably relate to.

Humans, of course, clearly have more sophisticated responses to violations of fairness. One of the most powerful examples of these is what psychologists call 'altruistic punishment'.

The test to demonstrate this involves a simple game: on each turn, players can choose to put an amount of money in a common pot.[4] The value of the pot is then increased (doubled, for example), and the resulting increased funds are then shared between all players equally. Critically, every player receives a share from the pot, even if they didn't pay into it. That means that some players can get a 'free ride'. They don't contribute, but they do benefit.

If you're anything like the players of the game, you'll already be feeling a bit annoyed that anyone could choose to be a free rider in this situation. It seems participants get sufficiently annoyed that, when offered the chance, they will give up some of their own money to punish them. For example they might pay £1 (that they will never see back) to have £1 taken from participants who are not contributing.

This concept of the 'altruistic' payment-to-punish is hard to explain if you believe that humans are purely rational and selfish. You could argue that participants were being rational if they thought that the punishment could pay off in the next round of the game, signalling to the free rider that they expected them to contribute in the next round. The behavioural economists who developed the game were concerned about that interpretation, so they included a condition where people could pay to punish even when they never expected to play the game or encounter the other players again. People still paid to punish free riders.

Researchers have carried out this experiment with people from cultures around the world (something psychologists don't do enough), with the same basic pattern of results. The extent to which individuals will pay to punish differs between cultures; however, the findings suggest that we are not simply motivated by a narrow sense of self-interest but that we have evolved to have a moral reaction to the idea that others aren't contributing fairly. (Interestingly, research has also shown that letting people punish others in group situations of this kind does ultimately result in better cooperation over time.[5] It seems that punishment can sometimes be an effective way to ensure groups work together.)

This research helps to explain why there are some political choices where we tend to agree. In essentially every democracy across the globe, we have a collective understanding that violations to certain rules should be punished. There is almost universal agreement, for example, that there should be some sort of penalty for those found guilty of theft, and as a result of this consensus these kinds of issue are not seen as hugely 'political'.

But beyond this, politics offers plenty of scope for disagreement. Recent elections in America, Britain and France, and the rise of nationalist parties across most of Western Europe, indicate that – in some countries at least – populations are becoming increasingly politically polarised. In 2014 the Pew Research Center conducted the largest political survey in its history – a poll of more than 10,000 adults – and concluded that Republicans and Democrats were 'further apart ideologically than at any point in recent history'.

Why are we so divided? Political and economic issues, like the 2008 financial crash and the increasing waves of migration across Europe, obviously play a large role. But part of what makes these issues so decisive is the way they tap into our different moral sensitivities. This is arguably one of the main obstacles to political dialogue: our views on controversial and changing issues such as tax, welfare or nationalism may depend upon intuitions that we cannot explain to others because we are not aware of them ourselves.

$\boxed{\times}$

This brings us to one of the most politically and morally charged issues of our time: inequality. In 2015 an Organisation for Economic Co-operation and Development (OECD) report identified the UK and the USA as two of the most unequal developed nations in the world. It warned that rising levels of inequality risked damaging the fabric of society as well as stunting economic growth. In 2014 Pope Francis tweeted: 'Inequality is the root of social evil', while Barack Obama has argued that inequality is 'the defining challenge of our time'.

Yale psychologist Paul Bloom recently examined our beliefs about economic inequality.[6] With colleagues Christina Starmans and Mark Sheskin, he argued that although the concept gets a lot of attention, when we look carefully at our responses to different situations, we don't disagree with inequality in and of itself. What we are concerned about is something that is often mistakenly conflated with inequality: economic unfairness.

Having reviewed a wide range of studies, they claimed the research shows that people prefer 'fair' distributions to equal ones.

If that distinction isn't clear, picture this scenario. Imagine you are a teacher helping a group of students with a project, and you become aware that some of the children are working much harder than others; essentially some of the children aren't really contributing to the project at all. Would you feel it was fair to assign the same grade to all of the children for the project, when you knew that this overall grade didn't reflect the individual efforts of each child?

Based on this idea, Bloom and his colleagues argue that we shouldn't focus on inequality but on *proportionality*, and whether wealth distribution fairly reflects different people's contributions. In short, they think we don't really mind if some people are paid in celery and others are paid in grapes – as long as we feel the people being paid in grapes deserve it.

If they are correct, then voters on both left and right should be able to tolerate a certain amount of inequality, provided they feel everyone has been treated fairly.

Simple? Not quite. For a start, who defines what is fair?

Unlike the general consensus on 'altruistic punishment', not all societies have the same customs or conventions about fairness. Children are able to pick up on these from a young age, as shown by some interesting cross-cultural studies by American psychologist Michael Tomasello.

In his work he showed that children quickly learned rules for what was right and wrong in particular contexts. In one experiment, children were taught how to play a game: one of the rules was that one event in the game had to happen before another event.[7] They were then introduced to a teddy who tried to play the game, but got things in the wrong order. The kids were not happy. They had not only learned what the rule was; they rapidly enforced that rule (with an earnest sense of right and wrong) when they saw the teddy violating it. You might recognise this earnest enforcement of rules from playing with your own kids: 'No, you don't do it like that!'

This research offers an interesting perspective on the way in which children are acutely sensitive to the social conventions around them. In the run-up to the EU referendum, for example, my seven-year-old niece was intensely interested in understanding who was 'right' and 'wrong'. Walking around Cambridge a month before the referendum she noticed the many Remain signs in people's gardens, and earnestly wanted to know if they were the 'good side'. Clearly she didn't understand what was actually being decided, but still she was trying to figure out the norms for her social group.

Tomasello's findings led him to predict that in different environments children might have different concepts of fairness. To test this he devised another simple game about the sharing of rewards.[8]

He tested children from a predominantly meritocratic culture (Germany) and from two African tribes, one highly egalitarian and one highly gerontocratic (where elders were in charge of making decisions). The children, playing in pairs, had to extract cubes from a container and were rewarded for how many cubes they collected. They then had to decide how those rewards would be shared (with no adults in sight).

The German kids were much more likely to share the rewards based on how well each child had done on the test, whereas the children from the egalitarian culture were more likely to share them equally. Children from the gerontocratic culture were rather idiosyncratic in how they shared the rewards (just respecting your elders doesn't seem to help kids learn a consistent notion of fairness!). The children spontaneously stuck to the ideas of fairness inherent in their culture, suggesting that evolution equips us with a propensity to learn about the concept of fairness, but doesn't necessarily dictate what version of fairness we will come to believe in.

☒

While concepts of fairness might differ around the world, most Western societies, like Germany, have a predominantly meritocratic notion of fairness, but that still doesn't mean people within those societies agree on what is fair – nor does it help us understand why they vote the way they do. To do that we need to delve deeper into the assumptions people make about why things are the way they are.

Let's go back to economic inequality: do you attribute someone's wealth to the actions of that individual or their circumstances in life?

Generally speaking, in America Republicans are much more likely to think that differences in wealth are a direct reflection of the amount of work put in, while Democrats believe that wealthier people tend to have had more advantages in life than others.[9]

This could explain why some of us support more generous welfare programmes (because people are poor for reasons beyond their control) and some of us oppose higher taxation policies for the rich (they are only rich because they have worked harder).

Why do we see things so differently depending on our political outlook?

The answer to this isn't totally clear, but there are a few clues. One very basic observation is that those on the left (at least in surveys in the USA) tend to have a slightly more accurate perception of how large the differences in equality are.[10] It's hard to say why this is: does their heightened concern for inequality make them more likely to be aware of the issue, or does their slightly more accurate perception of the issue make them more concerned about it?

Another helpful way to think about the fairness of inequality comes from the work of US political scientist John Alford and colleagues. Having researched whether our political views are determined by genetics, they found evidence that genetic make-up is in fact more important than environmental or familial factors.[11] They went on to argue that we should rethink how we talk about left and right or liberals and conservatives, to try to more accurately characterise the underlying psychological differences between them. They claim it is more helpful to think about two types of thinking style: 'contextual' vs 'absolute'.

Absolutist thinkers are more likely to see something as inherently right or wrong, whereas contextualist thinkers are more likely to allow for circumstances that could have influenced someone's behaviour.

Is there any evidence to support this way of categorising people? Well, let's take a look at different attitudes to punishment on the left and right – like inequality, this is a moral issue where we make intuitive judgements about what's fair.

As we've seen, although people tend to agree that certain moral violations should be punished, we often disagree on the nature of those punishments. For example, those on the political right are more likely to support the use of the death penalty than those on the left.

Fascinatingly, whether or not people support capital punishment is linked to whether they think the crime is a result of the individual's character or their circumstances.[12] In a similar way to how they account for wealth or poverty, conservatives (or absolutists) are more likely to hold the individual responsible for their own actions and view the death penalty as justified, while liberals (or contextualists) tend to point to mitigating circumstances or contextual factors and oppose the death penalty. Tony Blair famously moved the UK Labour Party closer to the centre of British politics by acknowledging both of these perspectives on crime when promising to be both 'tough on crime, and tough on the causes of crime'.

Interestingly, conservatives (absolutists) and liberals (contextualists) also seem to differ when it comes to the factors that influence human behaviour. Voters on the right are more likely to think that behaviour and personality are determined by genes,[13] whereas those on the left favour contextual factors like our upbringing or environment. So if you lean to the right, you may be more inclined to agree with Alford that your political choices might be influenced by your genes.

Our intuitions about what is fair – economically, or in terms of punishment – seem to be related to this underlying psychological difference: a style of thinking we might not even be aware of.

In 2012, Barack Obama gave a speech in which he said: 'If you've got a business, you didn't build that.' That phrase was taken out of context, but his point was that, if you have a business that transports goods, you didn't build the roads; if you rely on educated workers, you didn't educate them yourself. As Obama continued, 'If you've been successful, you didn't get there on your own', but relied on a system 'that allowed you to thrive'. You may well have worked hard, but that can't explain success on its own, because there are plenty of people out there who work hard. Perhaps it is a little clearer now why this 'contextual' argument would have resounded well with those on the left, but proved controversial to the right.

$$\boxed{\times}$$

These intuitions – and the way we think about individuals and their contexts – are also connected to our views on all kinds of topics, including immigration.

According to the absolutist/contextualist framework, those who are more likely to oppose immigration are also more likely to think that we all have a relatively fixed character that determines how we behave. So far this has only been demonstrated in Australia,[14] but it suggests that this is one of the reasons some people are more opposed to immigration, because they think immigrants might find it hard to adjust or integrate to a new society, which might result in tension or a lack of social cohesion.

But this is only a small part of it. To really understand controversial topics like immigration and nationalism, we have to look at what else shapes our morality.

Social psychologist Jonathan Haidt has argued that it's not just fairness we humans have developed a sensitivity to; there are all sorts of other factors, such as how we feel about the social groups we are part of (our ingroups) and our attitudes towards authority.

We've seen why we might have developed a sense of fairness; it is not quite so clear what has driven us to develop traits such as group loyalty. But again, it may come down to our selfish genes trying to get into the next generation.

Perhaps at some point in our evolutionary history, our survival (and that of our genes) was critically dependent on the survival of our group. For thousands of years, humans tended to live in small groups that relied on collaborative activities such as hunting and gathering, and, of course, fighting against other small groups. The way our behaviour evolved during that time could well have shaped the way we think about politics today.

Whether or not this theory is correct, Haidt has collected a range of evidence from a variety of countries, including the USA, UK and Canada, that suggests people who identify as left and right wing differ substantially in the way they see two key moral principles: group loyalty and respect for authority.[15]

Haidt and his colleagues found that people who identify as conservative are more likely to endorse statements like: 'Loyalty to one's group is more important than one's individual concerns' and 'The government should strive to improve the well-being of people in our nation, even if it sometimes happens at the expense of people in other nations'. They argue this reflects the greater moral emphasis conservatives place on loyalty to one's in-group, alongside other values including fairness, protecting people from harm and respect for authority.

By contrast, they find evidence that liberals only really emphasise two moral values: fairness and protecting people from harm. So liberals are less likely to agree that 'Loyalty to one's group is more important than one's individual concerns', but do tend to endorse statements such as: 'Justice, fairness and equality are the most important requirements for a society' and 'Compassion for those who are suffering is the most crucial value'.

This doesn't mean that conservatives are 'more moral' than liberals, just that they display moral sensitivities about a wider range of topics.

This difference could help us to understand the reasons behind the rising tide of nationalism around the world in recent years, and why it is such a polarising issue.

With the UK voting to leave the European Union, Donald Trump promising that 'from this day forward, it's going to be only America first', and Marine Le Pen's Front National achieving a historic share of the vote in France's presidential elections, we are witnessing a resurgence in nationalist sentiment. But while some of us rally behind nationalist politicians and policies, others are actively put off by them. Perhaps this is partly because we disagree over how important it is to be loyal to one's in-group. If the idea of putting your country first speaks to you – or, conversely, leaves you cold – the reason could lie in your moral values.

If conservatives have a broader range of moral intuitions than liberals, do right-wing parties have a political advantage? It is possible. They share moral concerns about fairness with those on the left (even if they may disagree on what is 'fair') but can also appeal to moral values that may be neglected by the left, such as nationalism. Interestingly, one of the few left-wing parties to have made significant gains in recent years is the Scottish National Party, which after years in the political wilderness managed to combine their policies on improved state welfare and free student tuition with the promotion of a sense of national identity.

If we look at the Brexit referendum in 2016, immigration and nationalism were clearly central issues, and I suspect moral intuitions played a huge role in determining how people voted. In the past, left-wing parties have frequently failed to address people's concerns over these issues. Professor Tariq Modood at Bristol University is very critical of the left for this reason, and argues that it has basically given the right a free hand to set the agenda on nationalism, rather than trying to develop its own positive vision.

Dismissing concerns about national identity or immigration as racist or nationalistic may or may not be fair, but it certainly doesn't seem to be helping the left win any arguments. This sense of dismissal (and its consequences) is perhaps epitomised in Hillary Clinton's famous description of many of Trump's supporters as a 'basket of deplorables'.

The various moral sensitivities that shape our political outlook are not easy to pinpoint or explain to others. Sometimes we don't even know ourselves why we intuitively think something is right or wrong. But understanding that our outlooks are based on some crucial differences in the way we interpret concepts of fairness, for example, can help us not only to understand the political choices we make, but also to try to comprehend the choices made by people with opposing views. You might still disagree, but at least it might be a little clearer what you are disagreeing about.

2

PERSONAL POLITICS

At 8 p.m. on Sunday 7 May 2017, Marine Le Pen, leader of the far-right party Front National, telephoned Emmanuel Macron to concede defeat in a presidential election that had changed the face of politics in France. Macron, who had formed his centrist party En Marche! only twelve months previously, swept to victory in a battle that seemed to transcend France's traditional left versus right party system.

Having eliminated the major candidates of both left and right in the first round, Macron and Le Pen then pitched their alternative visions for the future of France to a disparate and divided electorate. Foremost on the agenda were nationalism, internationalism, immigration and the EU. In a campaign speech Le Pen described this new political landscape as a battle between 'patriots and globalists'.

Two outsiders had redefined the French political landscape, reflecting ongoing political and economic changes seen across the Western world that are challenging the traditional distinctions between left and right.

As the BBC's Mark Easton argued: 'Conservative and Labour, left and right, capitalism and socialism – these ideological movements were a response to the economic and cultural challenges of power moving from the field to the factory. But power is moving again, from the national to the multinational. How citizens think we should respond to that shift is the new divide in our politics. It is less about left v right and more about nationalism v globalism.'

Easton is right that the ideological basis for the left and right is shifting. In the UK, for example, socio-economic class is now a much weaker predictor of which way people will vote. However, the psychological profile behind left- and right-wing voters can still help us to understand this new political landscape; indeed, when you take the underlying psychological profile into account, the divide between patriots and globalists might not be so unexpected.

$\boxed{X}$

As a psychologist, I'm constantly astonished by just how much we can predict about a person if they describe themselves as left or right wing (or liberal or conservative). It doesn't always enable us to know exactly which political policies that person will support, but we can make some reasonable guesses about their personality, moral values (as discussed in Chapter 1) – and even the size and activity of particular parts of their brain.

The origin of the terms 'left' and 'right' can be traced back to the French Revolution, when, in the newly established National Assembly, those supporting the king (and the established social order) would sit to the right of the chamber, and those advocating change would sit to the left. 'Right wing' and 'left wing' have since been used around the world to distinguish between supporters of 'stability and social order' on the right, and those in favour of 'change and reform' on the left. This distinction between a conservative party on the right and a party of change on the left still offers one of the most useful frameworks for understanding the main political fault lines in democracies around the world.[1]

Of course the specifics – the actual politics of left and right – vary from place to place. For example, in the UK or USA the right-wing parties are usually more enthusiastic about the free market, whereas in Eastern European countries that have moved away from communist rule, some parties on the left tend to be much more open to free-market capitalist policies, possibly because in these former communist states the move to the free market requires greater openness to change and reform. Even within the same country, context can be all-important: in the USA, for example, if someone says they are more liberal or conservative (roughly equivalent to left and right), their views might well depend on how 'blue' (Democratic) or 'red' (Republican) their state is.[2] In Texas a person who identifies as a Democrat may not support very liberal policies such as abortion or gay marriage, which a voter in California might see as key points on the Democratic agenda.

The fact that the left–right divide has offered a useful framework over the centuries and in different countries suggests that it has important roots in our psyche, in ways that might even be shared across cultures.

What could that mean?

Well, let's start with the basics: our genes. There seems to be something in our genetic make-up that predisposes us to be more left wing or right wing. For nearly fifty years, scientists have been studying identical twins to try to understand how much of their character or preferences comes from their genes, and how much comes from their environment.[3] Identical twins have the same genetic code, so we can say with more certainty that similarities are likely to come from their genes (although, crucially, only if they haven't grown up together). Overall, we've found that identical twins (raised separately) are more likely to share political views than non-identical twins. They don't always have the same views, of course, but there's enough similarity to suggest that, on everything from immigration to abortion to patriotism, having the same genes makes us more *likely* to agree.

In fact the correlation between having similar genes and having similar political beliefs is probably one of the most robust and replicated findings in political psychology, and one that holds true across a large number of countries.[4] However, it still isn't clear exactly how our genes influence our political beliefs – or our psychological traits and beliefs more generally. There are some clues, though: we can actually see differences in the brains and the physiological responses of people on different ends of the political spectrum.

In December 2010 the actor Colin Firth arrived as guest editor for BBC Radio 4's current affairs programme *Today* with a burning question: are there any differences in the brains of people who are left wing and right wing? Along with the BBC's science correspondent,

Tom Feilden, he asked Geraint Rees from University College London's Institute of Cognitive Neuroscience to investigate.

Rees initially carried out MRI scans on the brains of Conservative MP Alan Duncan and Labour MP Stephen Pound, and a sample of ninety young adults. He found that, surprisingly, the answer was yes: there were observable differences in the brains of those who identified as left or right wing. In fact, Rees could predict whether participants identified as liberal or conservative with around 70 per cent accuracy just by looking at the size and activity of two key parts of the brain: the amygdala and the anterior cingulate cortex (ACC).[5]

So, how do those areas of the brain function?

The amygdala, an almond-shaped part of the brain, has become quite well known in recent years. If you look online you will find people (a little misleadingly) calling it the 'lizard brain' because it seems to have developed very early in our evolution (other mammals have an amygdala too, and we think it has some similar functions in their brains). It's commonly associated with 'fear' but it's more complex than that – it helps us process and remember emotions, as well as shaping our perception of threats. It's so fundamental to how we perceive threats that a relatively direct connection from the eyes to the amygdala allows it to identify a threat before the rest of the brain has had a chance to even recognise what it's seeing.[6]

Brain scans have shown that both size and activity in the amygdala varies widely in different people.[7] In a paper titled 'Red Brain, Blue Brain', a group of researchers led by Darren Schreiber of the University of Exeter wanted to look at how the brains of liberals and conservatives differed when presented with a risk-taking scenario: a simple gambling game in which they had to choose between a lower 'safe' pay-off and a higher 'risky' pay-off.[8] They found that, while left-wing people and right-wing people didn't make different kinds of decisions, their brain activity was different: for those on the right, the amygdala was much more active. The conclusion was clear: how we deal with risk is closely related to how we respond to threat and conflict, and the greater activity in the amygdala shows that conservatives have a different cognitive process for thinking about risk, making them more sensitive to potential threats.

A similar discovery was made when observing physiological reactions. Our brains *and* our bodies show different responses, on average, depending on our political beliefs.

In 2008 a group of researchers led by Douglas R. Oxley at the University of Nebraska-Lincoln tested a number of people's 'galvanic skin responses' by using electrodes to pick up changes in the electrical current on their skin (the same technology forms a key part of the polygraph used in lie-detector tests).[9]

When presented with something perceived as a threat, an involuntary response takes place in our bodies, driven by electrical signals in the nervous system initiated by parts of the brain (including the amygdala). Though everyone has these basic response patterns, our individual sensitivity to threats varies widely. Oxley wanted to know if those variations might be related to our political views.

After finding out whether a sample of people supported a range of more liberal or conservative policies, the team showed them a series of pictures, which included three threatening images: a very large spider on the face of a frightened person, a dazed individual with a bloody face and an open wound with maggots in it – images we can well imagine might provoke an involuntary response, especially when we're not expecting them. Oxley and his colleagues found that those who supported more conservative policies showed a higher galvanic skin response than those who supported liberal policies.

All of this seems to suggest that those on the right are more sensitive to threats. But, what of those on the left?

In 2012, Oxley's colleague John Hibbing replicated his findings on how liberals and conservatives responded to threatening images.[10] But he wanted to go a step further. His team showed people similar negative images – a spider on someone's face, an open wound with maggots on it and a crowd fighting with a man – but this time he also included three positive images: a happy child, a bowl of fruit and a cute rabbit.

The researchers found that conservatives reacted more strongly to the threatening images, as before. But they also found that liberals had a stronger physiological response to the *positive* images. So, when they saw the 'happy' pictures of the rabbit or the child, they had a stronger involuntary reaction than the conservatives did.

As well as measuring skin responses, the study also used eye-tracking software to see exactly how much attention subjects were giving to the positive or negative pictures. They showed both kinds of images at the same time, to see which the participants were most drawn to, and how long they looked at them for.

Given that those on the right had a stronger response to the threatening images, the researchers wanted to see if that meant they'd be more or less inclined to look at those images. What they found was that conservatives were more likely to focus on the negative stimuli, whereas – you guessed it – the liberals' attention was drawn to the positive.

They concluded: 'the political left rolls with the good and the political right confronts the bad' – and, in fact, that's the title of the paper they wrote to explain their research.

It's a striking difference – but there's more. Coming back to Geraint Rees and Colin Firth's study, you might recall that the anterior cingulate cortex (ACC) also uncovered differences between conservatives and liberals: the studies showed it is more active in liberals when they're carrying out certain tasks.

The ACC is an area of the brain associated with decision-making and cognitive control. Crucially, we use it when we need to put in a bit of effort to carry out a task that requires a degree of flexible cognitive control.

In 2007 a group of researchers led by David Amodio at New York University set out to test the activity of the ACC in liberals and conservatives. They did this with a basic test called a 'Go/No Go' task, in which subjects had to rapidly press a button when they saw a signal, for example a red circle, but not press if that signal altered at all, for example, if it became a red square.[11]

Measuring people's accuracy and reaction times, they found that liberals made fewer errors, and that at certain points during the task, the ACC was more active in liberals than conservatives. This flexibility in their responses – based in the ACC – shows a striking correspondence to the more general flexible attitude that liberals tend to take to social issues.

What does all this tell us?

Well, in the simplest terms, it shows that there is a link between size and activity in certain parts of the brain, physiological responses and people's attitudes to society and politics.

But, as with so many interesting connections in science, we can't definitively say at this stage that one thing *causes* the other, just because we've seen a correlation. For example, we might think that conservatives naturally have a larger amygdala, and that makes them more sensitive to threats. But how much we use certain parts of our brain can also influence the size of those areas.[12] So, it might be that conservatives have a larger amygdala because they tend to focus more on threats, not vice versa.

Either way, the evidence points to a clear difference in how people interpret and respond to the world. And these physical differences do seem to relate in meaningful ways to our political leanings. If we have an increased sensitivity to threat, we might naturally view the world as a more dangerous place, so could be inclined to prioritise values like group loyalty and respect for authority. That could lead to support for increased spending on law and order, curbs on immigration, support for traditional values (such as those relating to family and religion) and stronger penalties for those who break the law.

In fact, researchers in the Netherlands have indeed found that there is a close correlation between the extent to which people view the world as a dangerous place, and the extent to which they think things like group loyalty and respect for authority are important moral principles.[13]

So maybe the *moral* differences we've seen on the left and the right have some roots in the way our brains and bodies respond to how dangerous we think the world is. Perhaps those on the right are biased to overemphasise threats – but we might also argue that those on the left are biased to neglect certain threats. For example, returning to the French Revolution, conservative thinkers at the time such as Edmund Burke – and indeed many conservative thinkers subsequently – argued that those calling for change often underestimated the potential threats to society when change happens too rapidly, especially in times of revolution or social upheaval. It could well be that being more aware of potential threats, and prioritising values such as loyalty and respect for authority are important for social cohesion.

Whatever the causal direction, it seems clear that on issues like immigration or terrorism, those on the left do have a tendency to see less of a threat than those on the right. The science doesn't say whether this is a good or bad thing, or suggest anyone is right or wrong in their perceptions; but it can make us more aware of the different ways we are likely to respond to different social and political issues.

☒

Advanced neuroimaging techniques and subtle measures of physiological responses to threat can reveal a lot about the psychology of those on the left or the right. But we don't need an expensive brain scanner to understand many of the differences; we can tell a great deal simply by looking at the answers to a questionnaire.

If you've ever taken a personality test – maybe as part of a job interview or in an experiment – you might ask whether a simple questionnaire can really tell you much about who you are and how you make decisions.

The short answer is that it depends on the questions! There is actually a very serious science behind the design of questionnaires. If you get the questions (and response options) right, they can provide a meaningful measure of someone's character, and they can certainly tell us quite a lot about how someone is likely to vote.

Psychologists have been trying to find a reliable way of mapping a person's personality since the 1880s, and throughout the twentieth century many different theories were put forward as a way of categorising our various traits – with some doubting that there was even such a thing as 'personality'.

Psychologists came to recognise that people do have stable personality traits that can help explain how they respond in a range of different situations. Based on this, in the 1980s a psychologist called Lewis Goldberg coined the term 'Big Five' to describe the main ways in which our personality might differ, and this has become the most widely used and reliable academic tool for measuring personality.

The Big Five breaks personality down into five components (with the helpful acronym OCEAN):[14]

Openness to new experiences: original, imaginative, broad interests and curious (the opposite might be conventional or uncreative in outlook)

Conscientiousness: careful, thorough, diligent and self-controlled (the opposite might be disorganised, careless and impulsive)

Extraversion: sociable, fun-loving, self-assured, friendly and talkative (as opposed to quiet and reserved)

Agreeableness: empathetic, altruistic, trusting and warm

(as opposed to mistrustful, callous, uncooperative, stubborn and rude)

Neuroticism (which is sometimes given the alternative label 'emotional stability'): worrying, self-conscious and temperamental (the opposite would be calm and emotionally stable)

Each person receives a low or high score in each category, and combined, these give an overall picture of their personality. You can try the test for yourself online.* This test is used widely by psychologists in a wide range of contexts, from developing new models for organisational management to trying to understand why we vote the way we do.

This might at first seem counter-intuitive, but when you think about it, it doesn't seem unreasonable that our personality could have an effect on our political choices.

John Mayer, professor of psychology at the University of New Hampshire, sums this up very neatly: 'Our votes are an expression not only of which candidates are best – the Republicans, Democrats, or those candidates of another party – but also of our own way of perceiving and thinking about the world and what is good or bad

* For example, at the University of Cambridge's Psychometric Centre: discovermyprofile.com/tag/Personality

about it. Our personal perceptions and thoughts in this area (and others) have been shaped over time within our personalities.'[15]

What researchers have found is that – taking into account all the other factors such as class, race, geography and so on – there are a couple of striking differences in the personalities of people who are conservative or liberal. So much so, that if a person identifies as left or right wing we can make a reasonable guess about certain aspects of their personality.

The aspect in which liberals and conservatives differ the most is in their openness to new experiences. Not surprisingly, liberals rate themselves as higher on Openness than conservatives (this is true for both social and economic liberals).[16] This means that they tend to respond more positively to change and uncertainty, which, in practice, might mean they are more likely to want to change what they perceive as social inequality, support minority rights and welfare, and be more tolerant of complexity.

After Openness, the second most reliable difference is in Conscientiousness, on which conservatives score more highly. This means they might be more diligent and careful (e.g. in appearance, or in their work), with greater respect for convention and tradition, perhaps being more likely to defend the status quo and support religious and traditional values. Meanwhile, liberals can be a little disrespectful towards established norms and conventions – for example, a recent analysis of the social media site Twitter found that liberals were more likely to swear.[17]

After Openness and Conscientiousness, the results become less clear, but in some studies there is a trend for Neuroticism to be higher among those on the left, and for Extraversion to be higher on the right.

In the USA there is now a fairly well-established link showing that if a person is a strong liberal or conservative voter, they're likely to score more highly on either Openness or Conscientiousness, and researchers have found a similar trend in many other countries too. This was certainly the predominant pattern in a survey of the 2016 presidential election in the USA, which showed that, yes, those who scored highly on Openness were more likely to vote for Hillary Clinton, while those who scored highly on Conscientiousness were more likely to vote for Donald Trump. They also found that those with higher Neuroticism (low emotional stability) were more likely to vote for Clinton.[18] That might be because people who score more highly on Neuroticism will value the safety net of social security, and would be more likely to vote for a party supporting that.

What all of this shows us is that personality and political choices are linked – and the relationship is *probabilistic.* It may be more likely that a person who is more open to new experiences will have liberal viewpoints, but they could always adopt a conservative political ideology. It simply means that if you have a certain political outlook, you are *more likely* to have certain personality traits, moral intuitions and cognitive biases.

So, based on personality profile, I can make a guess as to someone's political leanings (and vice versa), and it's likely that I'd be right more often than I'm wrong.

Political campaigners are already wise to the possibilities. As more sources of data become available, the curious correlation between how we vote and our personality and life choices is becoming more and more apparent in everything from the way we use Twitter, to the posts we like on Facebook, to the books we order on Amazon (astoundingly, even when it comes to books about science, liberals and conservatives in the USA prefer different books:[19] liberals tend to go for general science such as physics and astronomy, while conservatives favour more specific subjects such as medicine or geophysics; in fact the only topic of equal interest to both is dinosaurs!). This has led to fears that the tell-tale signs left by our digital footprints are increasingly being used by political campaigns to target voters based on their personality profile, as we will see in Chapter 7.

$\boxed{X}$

If research shows that there are clear differences between voters on the left and right, how does this affect our present politics?

First, a couple of caveats:

Of course the picture we've painted of left and right wing is a simplification – in reality things are always more complex. Libertarians in the USA, for example, seem to have a different kind of 'third' psychological profile. Social psychologist Jonathan Haidt has argued that libertarians don't fit into the moral profiles of either liberals or conservatives, emphasising, for example, the importance of individual liberty above all other moral concerns.[20]

So, if you don't feel that the psychological profiles we've looked at here apply to you, that makes sense – there's definitely more to it.

It also doesn't mean that our political views are fixed. Our personality can change over our lifetime, and so too can our politics. People often say that we become more conservative as we age – 'Any man who is under thirty, and is not a liberal, has no heart; and any man who is over thirty, and is not a conservative, has no brains,' as Winston Churchill supposedly said.

But while this does appear to have been true for the baby boomer generation, it isn't necessarily true for all generations in all contexts.[21] It does seem that as we get older the link between our genetics and our politics gets stronger.[22] That could be because at a younger age our politics are more influenced by our upbringing, but as we get into our twenties we become freer to make our own choices in life, and so our genetic tendencies are more readily expressed. As we've seen, that doesn't mean our genes literally determine our politics; rather, our genes might shape certain biases, and that in turn those biases increase the likelihood that we'll take a particular political stance.

So life experiences are hugely important, of course, as are the policies offered by particular parties. In the 2017 election in the UK, age and home ownership were two huge predictors of how people voted. This almost certainly can't be explained purely based on individual differences in people's personality, given that the Labour Party explicitly targeted the vote of younger generations (both in terms of voter registration and policies like free university tuition) and offered support for those renting (with further regulations on private renting).

Nevertheless, some of the individual differences on the left and the right offer a good starting point for understanding why we might respond to and interpret events differently.

These days, the ideological basis for left- and right-wing politics might be increasingly unclear; nevertheless some of the psychological differences we've looked at might help us to understand how people are responding to changing circumstances. Le Pen's formulation of a new divide between 'patriots' and 'globalists' actually follows quite logically from some of the main differences we have seen in the last two chapters. In the previous chapter, we saw how those on the right typically have a higher sense of in-group loyalty, which obviously accords with the 'patriots', those who feel comfortable putting their country first. In this chapter we have seen that cognitive flexibility and openness to new experiences is generally higher on the left, which again clearly accords with an openness to a changing globalised world. The left might therefore be psychologically inclined to be open to migrants from other cultures, and to changing relationships between countries, such as the increasing integration of the countries of the European Union.

These traits of in-group loyalty and openness to new experiences probably played a role in the recent UK referendum on membership of the EU. We know that British voters from across the political spectrum voted to leave the EU for a variety of reasons, but preliminary research suggests leave voters were, by and large, less open to new experiences, as measured by the Big Five.

If those on the right are less open to new experiences, we might not have predicted that predominantly right-wing voters would vote for the 'change' of leaving the European Union, thinking instead that the Remainers' message of 'Better Together' might have held more sway. However, mass migration from the EU, and the EU's right to impose laws on the UK meant that, for many voters, the EU was itself a source of change and instability. An enhanced sense of in-group loyalty also means that the importance of preserving 'British culture' is much more likely to appeal intuitively to those on the right than on the left. As we've seen, those on the right are more likely to be sensitive to potential threats, and this probably made them more sensitive to mass migrations. Maybe the fact that many on the left don't intuitively understand the perceived threat (justified or not) of immigration contributed to right-wing voters feeling that their concerns about the issue were not being listened to. And perhaps it also accounts for the popular success of a Leave campaign that promised to 'take back control' of national borders.

Similar language was used by Le Pen during the recent presidential election, when she claimed that French 'civilisation' was under threat. 'Give us France back, damn it!' she demanded at a rally in Paris while her supporters chanted: 'This is our home!' Pledging to suspend even legal immigration, she took aim at France's Muslim population: 'In France, we drink wine whenever we want. In France we do not force women to wear the veil because they are impure . . . In France, we get to decide who deserves to become French.'

Even though she didn't win, she still got a surprisingly large segment of the vote for a far-right party. With a greater understanding of the personality differences between voters, we can perhaps understand how her rhetoric about homeland, taking back borders, promising security and advocating nationalist economics as opposed to greater globalisation would appeal to conservatives, with their higher sensitivity to threats, their inclination toward in-group loyalty and their desire for stability.

We can see the same trends in politicians' speeches appealing to voters on the left. Democrat Barack Obama referred to his political platform as 'rejecting fear', and asked voters to 'choose hope'. Jeremy Corbyn, leader of the Labour Party in the UK, has often characterised his political agenda as one of hope, in contrast to the agenda of 'fear' advocated by his Conservative opponent Theresa May. Both men seem to be quite explicitly rejecting some of the psychological biases associated with the opposite side of the political spectrum.

Liberal commentators are frequently frustrated by sections of the electorate voting for a party or candidate that would appear to be against the voters' own interests (for example, working-class voters supporting a party that advocates lower taxes for the rich). American political psychologist John Jost suggests that what those on the left fail to understand is that voters on the right are not simply concerned about economic benefits; rather, some may be voting for policies that fulfil a broader cognitive need for continuity, order and a sense of national identity. Jost's view might also help to explain why countries tend to shift to the right in times of perceived threat. For example, after a terrorist attack, the heightened sense of anxiety seems to make ideas of in-group loyalty and national stability more important to many voters.

If we do vote, at least in part, according to our psychological needs, then it makes sense to find out more about what those needs, biases and impulses are and how they shape the way we view the world. That way we can form a better understanding of how we might respond as our political environment changes.

I've focused on the left–right axis here partly because we have so much interesting evidence for how it can help us to view our differences. Probably, over time, the study of political psychology will change, and we will develop different axes that describe us better (and there are lots of other ways academics have done that in the past, many of which have merit). But, for now, left and right are still a useful starting point for looking at political cultures.

Psychology can't tell us if a bias is right or wrong, but it might help us to understand why people hold particular views, sometimes so different to our own. That doesn't mean we all have to agree, but we can at least have a little more appreciation of each other's perspective – and perhaps a little more harmony around the dinner table at the next family gathering.

3

WHY YOU ALWAYS THINK YOU'RE RIGHT

In spring 2016, TV presenter and former Conservative MP Gyles Brandreth went to Guildford in Surrey, a traditionally conservative town and, as he puts it, 'capital of the Home Counties', with a list of political policies and a BBC camera crew in tow.

He wanted to discover whether the voters in Guildford, when presented with policies without knowing whether they were Labour or Conservative, would agree or disagree with them.

The mischievous Brandreth set out to find, as he puts it, 'secret socialists'. He posed a series of questions to passers-by, including:

'Would you like to see university fees scrapped and replaced with maintenance grants?'

'Would you support a fully funded NHS, integrated with social care, with an end to privatisation in healthcare?'

'Would you like to see private rents linked with local average earnings levels?'

'Are you in favour of restoring the 50 per cent tax rate on incomes over £150,000?'

Many of those interviewed enthusiastically agreed.

Brandreth then took great pleasure in revealing the source of the policies, whipping out a photograph of Labour leader Jeremy Corbyn – a man even members of his own parliamentary party see as standing for the far left.

Many of these Guildford shoppers were shocked, if not horrified, to find that they agreed with so many of Corbyn's 'socialist' policies, with exclamations of 'No!' and 'Terrible!'

One woman summed up her feelings, saying, 'Well, that is really frightening ... I think I'd better go back in my hole.' It seems that in this case, the *fact* that they agreed with the policy didn't match their *belief* that they support the Conservatives, not Labour (and especially not Jeremy Corbyn's brand of Labour). The thought that they might actually agree with the *other side* came as quite an unwelcome surprise.

But it's not hugely surprising when you know a bit more about how the human brain makes choices – and especially how it makes political choices.

Jimmy Kimmel ran a similar story in the USA, asking Americans if they preferred the Affordable Care Act or Obamacare. Many people were adamant that they preferred the Affordable Care Act, when in fact, they are the same thing – Obamacare is just its nickname. When one passer-by was asked why they didn't like Obamacare, they replied, 'Well, it's in the name, isn't it?'

These (entertaining) cases point to a divergence between how we feel about our political allegiance and which policies we actually prefer – a divergence that ultimately shapes how we vote.

We are not always the rational creatures we might think we are – weighing up options, judging all the evidence and coming to a considered conclusion. In fact, we are driven by a number of cognitive biases that can make us resistant to either facts or reason. These biases can affect our decision-making in all aspects of our lives – sometimes in a negative way, for example in shaping an aversion to a particular type of person, but often simply in a functional way that allows us to make quick, unconscious decisions while navigating our complex world.

In politics, three of these biases – cognitive dissonance, motivated cognition and confirmation bias – tend to convince us that we (or our group) are right, and make us resistant to seeing when we might be wrong.

We'll deal with them separately, but in reality they blend together – like a potent cocktail of biases, each with its own special flavour. Let's take a look at those ingredients.

$\boxed{X}$

Those 'secret socialists' in Guildford experienced some discomfort when they realised that their beliefs didn't match their party loyalty. And I'm sure we've all had moments when our perception of ourselves has been subject to some sort of challenge.

In such circumstances, we, like the shoppers, can respond in a number of ways: we can revise our beliefs, come up with excuses or justifications, or maybe just stubbornly ignore the evidence.

Brandreth's revelations were light and funny, but those shoppers would almost certainly have felt a moment of awkwardness when the contradiction was revealed.

In psychology we call this uncomfortable experience 'dissonance'. When faced with a seeming contradiction within your own beliefs, your unconscious mind immediately tries to find some way of reconciling that inconsistency in a process known as 'cognitive dissonance', and it sometimes results in us changing our beliefs without us even being aware of it. This idea was first developed in 1957 by American psychologist Leon Festinger in his influential book *A Theory of Cognitive Dissonance*. His work sparked thousands of subsequent studies and has influenced research in fields as diverse as advertising and healthcare.

Festinger had been intrigued by reports of an earthquake in the Bihar region of India in 1934. After the earthquake, wild rumours started to spread about further calamities that were about to befall the region – cyclones, floods and so on. People were scared – and so they spread rumours that would scare themselves even further. Why?

Festinger concluded that the rumours fulfilled a need: people wanted the world to match the fear they already felt. This insight led to his theory of cognitive dissonance: when our feelings and the facts don't match up, we'll find some way to make them match. In that way, we can overcome the uncomfortable feeling of disconnect – or 'dissonance'.

This is a really provocative theory. It suggests that the feeling of internal inconsistency was worse than the idea of further disasters, and therefore that people's beliefs could be shaped not just by reason and evidence but by this unconscious desire for consistency. The mind comes up with various strategies to deal with this: we might change our beliefs – or come up with justifications and rationalisations to explain the conflict.

In the simplest terms, it's a way of lying to ourselves to avoid things that we find it uncomfortable to confront.

Like all of the biases in this chapter, however, sometimes cognitive dissonance plays a very functional role in our lives. Imagine you are stuck in a job you don't like – perhaps you can't leave because it pays the bills, or because the thought of finding a new job seems overwhelming, or you see yourself as someone who always succeeds, and so the thought of giving up on this doesn't chime with your perception of yourself. Whatever the reason, rather than acknowledging how unhappy you are, you might (unconsciously) search for reasons why this job isn't really so terrible – it could be worse, after all, and at least you *have* a job, and you quite like your colleagues, and the hours are pretty good, and remember how much you enjoyed it in the beginning?

Years later, looking back on that time from the perspective of a new, different job, you might finally be able to admit to yourself that the previous job hadn't really been right for you. But at the time, this sort of unconscious reasoning might help you stick out a difficult situation, believing things aren't really all that bad and maintaining a positive view of yourself.

It's likely that one of the reasons we experience cognitive dissonance is because we are always trying to maintain a positive coherent idea of ourselves, i.e., keeping up a positive self-image, or telling ourselves that we're a rational and consistent person.

This idea of maintaining a coherent notion of ourselves can be very strong – so strong, in fact, that sometimes we change or update our beliefs just to maintain that image, even when it doesn't seem like the logical thing to do.

In one American study, researchers asked students to argue the case for or against a controversial topic. Afterwards, some participants stuck with the opinion they'd presented, even if it's not what they'd previously believed. But that's not necessarily because they found their own arguments so convincing. Some other students who were *paid* to argue the case were *less* likely to change their mind.[1]

It's possible that an unpaid person's (unconscious) reasoning in this experiment runs something like this: 'If I've put all this effort into arguing for this position, and I haven't been paid to do so, but I'm a rational, sensible person who uses their time wisely, then I obviously must genuinely support this position'. Whereas the other students already had a good justification for investing their time – getting paid – and viewed it as just a job.

You can see how it might be difficult to change

someone's mind once they've already spent a lot of their time arguing a political point!

We can also become very attached to groups – or parties – that we identify with, to the point where that group can become part of our own identity. When it comes to party politics, it seems that (as Gyles Brandreth's amusing fieldwork suggested) being consistent in how we identify with a group can sometimes be more important than our beliefs about specific policies.

Geoffrey Cohen, a professor of psychology at Stanford, revealed just how strong – and unconscious – this tendency is.[2] In 2003, he asked Democrats and Republicans what they thought of a particular welfare policy. They divided clearly and predictably along party lines: the Democrats preferred a more generous welfare reform, and the Republicans a more financially prudent policy.

Then he asked a new group what they thought of these policies – but this time he told them it was either a Democratic or Republican policy.

Knowing they were 'party' policies, Democrats were more likely to approve of the prudent welfare package, and Republicans to approve of the generous 'Republican' welfare reform.

Perhaps this isn't so surprising – political parties switch their policies around all the time. Before the 2015 UK general election, for example, the left of centre

Labour Party argued that they wanted to raise the mini-mum wage; once the election was over, the Conservative Party then announced a major policy shift and decided to support the same measure.

But when Cohen asked those people whether they were influenced by the fact that the policy was labelled Republican or Democrat, they thought they were not! (Interestingly, though, they thought that their adversaries would be. It seems that Democrats think Republicans are more likely to toe the party line; and vice versa.)

We don't generally realise that we're being influenced by a group allegiance – we think that our attitudes and judgements are impartial, an assessment of the facts. We prefer to see ourselves as objective and free of bias.

But there's a good reason why we might follow the group, without realising it – and it's not necessarily mindless conformity.

Maybe it makes good sense to rely on a political party. After all, who really has the time to reason through the detail of every policy proposal? Isn't it more straight-forward to have a degree of trust that other people in the party, whose views tend to be in line with yours, have done that already, so we can rely on their judgement?

But it is also a question of identity. Like Brandreth's shoppers, we might be very attached to the idea of ourselves as Republican or Democrat, Labour or

Conservative. And if that's the case, when we are presented with a policy that seems to contradict what we think the party stands for, perhaps it's simply easier to change our policy choices than face up to a challenge to our identity.

|X|

Another result of our tendency to succumb to cognitive dissonance is that we hate being wrong – and we'll find ways to avoid it, without even realising we are doing so.

In fact, some people aren't even sure what their views are, but are very quick to provide reasons and justifications, sometimes even for choices that they didn't make.

In one study, voters were asked their level of agreement on a large number of issues.[3] Afterwards, they were shown their choices and asked to justify them. However, the researchers had inserted a few trick questions – they had switched some of the respondents' views around. A surprisingly large number of people didn't even notice.

But perhaps more incredibly, of those who didn't notice the swap, a small number then went on to construct an argument as to why they supported that policy, when they'd initially said they supported the reverse.

It might seem absurd that people would give reasons in support of a policy that their initial response suggested they didn't support – but this in fact is something people do all the time. There are a whole range of situations in which we will happily offer up explanations for decisions we have made, despite not actually being aware of what the real reasons are. And, given that we don't like to make a wrong decision, we'll do everything we can to tell ourselves that we made the right choice the first time.

Let's take an example. When you enter a polling booth, you're usually fairly sure why you're going to vote for a particular candidate.

But it turns out that you're more sure *after* you've cast your vote.

A number of studies have found evidence of this in the real world, surveying people either before or after they've been in the voting booth in the USA[4] and Canada.[5] They found that voters were consistently more positive about their candidate after having voted.

Why would we be more certain afterwards? Maybe, when faced with the choice, all of the arguments for or against each candidate became crystal clear and we came to a rational decision at the moment of voting. Or, maybe, we just want to believe that we've made the right decision – we feel dissonance at any inkling that we might have chosen wrongly, so we work harder to justify it after the fact.

This desire to avoid being wrong has been shown to affect our voting preferences before the fact, too.

Stanford political psychologist John Jost has conducted a number of experiments to test this. In one, people were presented with a fabricated (but seemingly respectable) survey that suggested a Gore or Bush presidency was more likely in the 2000 US election.[6] Those who saw the survey suggesting Gore was about to win were more convinced a Gore presidency would be a good thing (and vice versa).

Rather than face the dissonance of being wrong, we seem to prefer to support whoever is likely to win. (As an aside, this experiment quite clearly shows that election polls are not just a measurement of people's opinion; they can actively influence it.)

This desire to avoid being wrong is closely related to another bias, which you are bound to have heard of if you've spent any time on the internet in the past few years: the now-infamous confirmation bias.

$\boxed{X}$

In September 2015, Angela Merkel, the German chancellor, was overheard in conversation with Facebook CEO Mark Zuckerberg at a United Nations function.

This was at the peak of the European refugee crisis; that same month Merkel had made the historic and controversial decision to open Germany's borders to up to a million refugees. Merkel confronted Zuckerberg about the proliferation of anti-immigration posts on Facebook in Germany, asking, 'Are you working on this?', with Zuckerberg responding that 'we need to do some work' on limiting their number.

In recent years the power that social media channels like Facebook and Twitter have to spread ideas and influence opinion has seen them identified as the driver of the political polarisation we've seen across Western democracies.

It is no coincidence that over the same period the phrase 'confirmation bias' has made it from obscure psychology articles into more common parlance. People have started to understand that the internet, and in particular social media, might supercharge our ability to seek out people and sources of information that support our current views – allowing us to create what have become known as 'filter bubbles'. There's speculation, too, that our tendency to create these bubbles has been amplified by the way companies like Google and Facebook select content that they think will be of most interest to us.

According to the Pew Research Center, 44 per cent of Americans and 61 per cent of millennials use Facebook as their primary source for news about politics and, because Facebook feeds are based on past clicks and likes, users are mostly shown political content that tallies with their own views. Social media systems like Facebook certainly aren't designed to expose users to opposing opinions, whereas a newspaper might deliberately hire a columnist with views contrary to the paper's (and readers') political stance, just to get a debate going.

Is it fair to say that social media is a prime driver of political polarisation?

Perhaps not. Researchers at Brown University in the USA recently found that the polarisation of views is largest among the elderly – the people least likely to use the internet or social media.[7] There are also reasons to think that in following friends and family on Facebook we are sometimes exposed to more counter-partisan views than we might otherwise encounter.[8] It looks likely then that social media is an influence on this phenomenon, but that it is just part of a bigger story.

So what exactly is confirmation bias, and how might it influence how we seek out and process information?

As a day-to-day example, anyone who watches football – or knows someone who does – will be familiar with the tendency of supporters to believe that their team is consistently fair, whereas the opposition are brutal cheats and the referee is clearly bent. Whatever the events of a particular match, opposing sets of fans seem able to recall a litany of incidents and perceived grievances to support their case.

Or, let's say that you and your partner disagree about who does most of the housework. The jobs that you do and the time and effort you expend on them will spring easily to mind, whereas the few chores you can remember your partner doing will fade into insignificance.

Or perhaps at work you might believe that your team always does more work than the others and always meets the deadlines. Of course, there might have been that one time you were a bit late with a project – but that was only because etc. etc. etc. ....

This sort of thinking is our confirmation bias, whirring away in the background of our brains to reassure us that everything is as it should be (or as we think it should be, anyway).

There isn't one single agreed definition of confirmation bias, but it is essentially the tendency to seek out evidence consistent with your ideas or values, and to resist or find reasons to discredit evidence counter to your existing beliefs.

As we have seen, this is something that people do frequently on social media, but psychologists have been talking about confirmation bias for a long time, and it's clear that it doesn't require an internet connection.

In fact, people have recognised this tendency throughout the ages. In 1620 the English scientist and philosopher Francis Bacon wrote: 'The human understanding when it has once adopted an opinion (either as being the received opinion or as being agreeable to itself) draws all things else to support and agree with it.'

More recently, here is a line from an influential psychological study published in 1979,[9] which stated that exposing different social groups 'to an identical body of relevant empirical evidence may not [result in] a narrowing of disagreement but rather an increase in polarisation'.

That sounds very familiar.

In that 1979 study, psychologist Charles Lord and his colleagues at Stanford University wanted to see how biased we can be when looking at factual evidence, so they chose an emotive topic that elicits strong views in the USA: the death penalty.

First they asked participants for their views on capital punishment, then they presented them with a range of arguments for and against. Having been given such a balanced range of information, we might have thought that some people would at least have softened their position – it's plausible that people might moderate their views when presented with a range of evidence. But the study tells us human reasoning sometimes just doesn't work like that.

The researchers found that people came away with even more extreme views than they had held before. Whatever their stance, the participants decided that all of the *important* evidence was in support of their own viewpoint, and found ways of discounting the evidence to the contrary.

Over the years, it has become clearer that confirmation bias is fairly ubiquitous across individuals and situations.[10] This means it affects pretty much all of us, and we're not yet completely sure why.

Francis Bacon's recognition of this tendency was integral to the development of the modern scientific method. Scientists need to be trained not only to run experiments and build theories, but also to think of tests or predictions that might prove those theories wrong. In proving ourselves wrong, we have to develop a new theory, and so our knowledge advances.

But the fact that scientists have to be specifically trained to look for evidence which contradicts their theories confirms it's not a process that comes naturally to us.

In the late 1980s, political scientist Philip Tetlock embarked on a major project that was to last nearly twenty years. He wanted to know how often 'experts' are right in their predictions.

Until 2003, he tracked the predictions of a number of experts – pundits, commentators, talking heads who get quoted in newspaper articles as experts, and so on – whose job it is to comment on and predict political and economic trends and events. The results were included in his book *Expert Political Judgment* in 2005.

First of all, he found that they are wrong more often than they're right (and that applied to TV experts in particular). And, second, he found that they weren't right any more often than an informed layperson would have been.

This might or might not surprise you depending on your opinion of experts and pundits.

But if that's the case, how could they possibly continue to be trusted as predictors – or, more importantly, how could they continue to believe in their own ability to predict?

Well, it turns out that these 'experts' are just like the rest of us. They don't like being wrong – and they'll intuitively look for all the reasons why they were right, or half-right, or could have been right under different circumstances.

Rather than learning from their mistakes, Tetlock's experts used the same cognitive tricks that we all use: they tended to focus more on the times when they got it right, and were a lot more critical of examples that contradicted their predictions.

✗

As we know, debates on social media can get very heated, each side seemingly shouting at the other across a chasm. We really don't like it when we're given evidence that challenges our deeply held beliefs. It's not just that we disagree with it, we seem to actively dislike it. That brings us to our third way of thinking: motivated cognition.

It's a form of what psychologists call 'hot' cognition – a description that makes sense when you consider how heated people can get about certain subjects like politics, religion or morality. It's similar to confirmation bias, but it's not just a 'cognitive' bias. It is deeply rooted in our emotions, our values, our identity – we're 'motivated', for example, to maintain a positive self-image or a belief system.

If you've ever had a political debate with your family at Christmas you probably have all the evidence you need that people can get emotional when they are defending their position. But in 2016, neuroscientists Jonas Kaplan, Sarah Gimbel and Sam Harris, knowing that people often ignore information that conflicts with their deeply held beliefs, wanted to see what was going on in our brains when this happened and conducted a functional MRI imaging experiment – with some interesting results.[11]

The study involved a group of liberals who said that they held their convictions deeply. While measuring the flow of blood in their brains, the researchers showed them a number of statements that confirmed their beliefs, such as 'Abortion should be legal' and 'Taxes on the wealthy should generally be increased'. The participants were then also shown a series of strong counter-arguments and, afterwards, they were asked to rate how strongly they agreed with the original statements.

A clear difference in brain activity emerged; those people with more fixed views showed more activity (as measured by an increased blood flow) in areas of the brain associated with emotional processing compared to those who were more able to change their minds.

Given the deep-seated emotional nature of our responses to information that challenges our beliefs, this is perhaps one of the most potent elements of the cocktail. It certainly helps to explain why debates can get so heated – and it shows why we might not be quite as rational as we think we are when it comes to political arguments.

$$\boxed{X}$$

We are all affected by our biases in our everyday lives. If you want to see how they might affect your reasoning when it comes to politics, there are an increasing number of websites that enable you to run a version of Brandreth's experiment on yourself. They ask you which policies you support, without telling you which party they are associated with, and then combine your policy preferences to let you know which party's policy platform you support the most. I'd be prepared to wager that if the party identified by the website doesn't match the party you support in real life, you'll experience some uncomfortable dissonance. I'd also wager that if they do match, you'll feel relieved, and maybe even a little elated, that you were 'right'.

The more we discover about these ways of thinking, the less clear the dividing line becomes between reason and emotion. In fact it might be that this dividing line is ill-conceived in the first place. Our decisions are often guided by how we feel, and in some instances those feelings help us make better choices. The idea that we would use only reason when making a decision has been described by Jonathan Haidt as a 'rational delusion', stating that 'emotions are information' in certain contexts.

So, the next time you get engaged in a political discussion, try to pay attention to what is going on in your own thoughts and emotions. You might notice your mind racing to find some evidence consistent with your own position, or you might catch yourself summarily dismissing a counter-argument, before you've even finished listening to the other person. You might also detect a little emotional turmoil when you hear an argument that is actually quite interesting, but that doesn't support your views.

If you do start feeling a little heated, that doesn't mean you're being irrational. Our emotional response is an important part of our identity and our perspective on the world, and it often plays a key role in the decisions we make. If, for example, you become passionate about a subject because it is important to how you think we can make the world a better place, then don't worry – that's a subject worth getting heated about. Paraphrasing philosopher David Hume, sometimes 'reason ought to be the slave to the passions'.

That said, you probably don't want to be a slave to all of your cognitive biases, at least not all of the time. It can be hard to know how much influence they are exerting on your decisions, but it's worth pausing to ask yourself the question any time you set about persuading people why they're wrong and you're irrefutably right.

4

WHAT'S IN A FACE?

We all know that first impressions matter – and that's especially true in politics. But would you vote for someone because of the way they look?

Well, as it turns out, you just might.

We make judgements based on people's appearance all the time. Mostly we're not even aware that we're doing it. Apart from obvious cues, like a punk hairstyle or a biker jacket, there are all sorts of ways we try to make sense of other people, coming to conclusions that help us to evaluate them – even just from looking at their face.

When we vote we think we're making a rational decision, but we could be influenced by something much less logical: a snap judgement – the kind you make in the blink of an eye.

Let's take one very famous example of how appearances matter: the first televised presidential debate in the USA between one-term senator Democrat John F. Kennedy and Eisenhower's vice-president and seasoned campaigner Republican Richard Nixon.

The decision even to broadcast this debate was extremely controversial at the time. Newspapers were the home of politics, whereas TV was considered a medium of entertainment. Journalist Theodore H. White warned that putting candidates on the spot on TV risked dumbing down politics altogether: 'Neither man could pause to indulge in the slow reflection and rumination, the slow questioning of alternatives before decision, that is the inner quality of leadership.' Others were concerned that it was a slippery slope that would turn political discourse into some kind of game show: 'If we test Presidential candidates by their talents on TV quiz performances, we will, of course, choose presidents for precisely these qualities,' said University of Chicago historian Daniel Boorstin.

Nevertheless, it went ahead.

The stakes could not have been higher: within the previous four years, Soviet tanks had crushed a democratic revolt in Hungary, the USSR had shocked the world with the successful launch of Sputnik, Fidel Castro had established his revolutionary regime in nearby Cuba, and domestically, the struggle for civil rights was dividing the nation. More than 90 per cent of American homes now had TV sets, and an estimated 70 million people tuned in to the contest.

With the rivals campaigning tirelessly throughout the summer of 1960, Nixon had inched ahead in the polls. Twice vice-president, he hadn't lost an election in over thirty years, and thought he would easily beat the handsome but callow forty-three-year-old Kennedy.

But, arriving at the studios, he banged his knee stepping out of the car (exacerbating an earlier injury), and having recently suffered a bout of the flu, he was still running a low fever. He'd also spent a gruelling day on the campaign trail. 'Nixon looked like warmed-over death. He'd been in the hospital, his color was bad ... He was not a well man,' recalled CBS president Frank Stanton. And yet, despite this, and despite confessing to Walter Cronkite in an interview two weeks earlier, 'I can shave within thirty seconds before I go on television and still have a beard,' Nixon declined the services of CBS's top make-up artist, who had been summoned from New York for the event. At his aides' urging, Nixon submitted only to a coat of Lazy Shave, a pancake make-up he had previously used to mask his five o'clock shadow.

Kennedy on the other hand had spent the day preparing with aides for the debate, and then had a nap. He too turned down the services of CBS's make-up artist, because he already had a perfect tan. Kennedy was more than ready for his close-up.

From the start of the debate it was clear that the young Democrat had found his moment to shine. Calm, knowledgeable and effortlessly handsome, his practice of looking at the camera when answering the questions – and not at the journalists who asked them, as Nixon did – made viewers feel he was talking to them, giving them straight answers. Pale and in pain, Nixon quickly started sweating under the hot studio lights, causing the Lazy Shave powder to melt off his face in beads of sweat, and his sideways glances at the studio clock – that the home audience couldn't see – had the added effect of making him look shifty. So catastrophic was the debate for Nixon that Chicago mayor Richard J. Daley reportedly said, 'My God, they've embalmed him before he even died.' The following day, the *Chicago Daily News* ran the headline 'Was Nixon Sabotaged by TV Makeup Artists?'

The debate is widely recognised as the turning point in Kennedy's campaign. ('It was TV more than anything else that turned the tide,' said Kennedy four days after the election.) And although some of that was because of what Kennedy said – he spoke with confidence and optimism about the issues that concerned voters – how he looked was certainly a big factor.

We know this because, despite the large viewing figures, many voters still chose to listen to it on the radio. And, while those that watched the debate on TV thought Kennedy was the clear winner, those who listened to the debate on the radio thought Nixon had won. Given how tight the election was – Kennedy won the popular vote 49.7 per cent to 49.5 per cent – this debate remains a fascinating example of the importance of appearance.

As far as experiments go, it's not perfect: it's possible that those listening to the debate on the radio might have been more likely from the start to prefer Nixon – perhaps, say, because they lived in rural areas where television had not yet reached. (Relatively few Catholics – a key Kennedy constituency – lived in the countryside.)

But this isn't the end of the story. In 2003 a researcher called James N. Druckman revisited the debate in an experiment, to find out whether people's opinions really were influenced by what they saw. He randomly assigned people to watch or listen to the recording, and then report on whether they thought Kennedy or Nixon had been more successful. The results were again quite clear: those who watched the debate, rather than listened to it, were much more likely to say they thought Kennedy won.[1] Something made people think Kennedy had come off better.

Nixon was ill, and he looked ill. But surely we understand that everyone gets ill now and then. If a politician can campaign for months, garnering support from party and public, and fine-tuning their policies, it hardly seems likely that our decision whether or not to vote for them will be based on, for example, the one time they have appeared in public feeling a bit under the weather. Surely that's not a rational way to go about choosing our leaders.

Part of the problem here is the idea of competence.

Competence is extremely important to voters – and rightly so. Of course we want our leaders to be competent! But we don't always come to a decision about competence rationally. In the Kennedy/Nixon example, the visual contrast between the two – and not what they were saying – was enough to give Kennedy a boost.

This is an extreme example. But, in fact, our judgements of 'competence' are often made in the blink of an eye – just by looking at a person's face. And those judgements aren't necessarily accurate.

A psychologist called Alexander Todorov wanted to investigate just how much we are influenced by these snap judgements.[2] He conducted an experiment in which he showed people photos of two politicians, and asked them to say which of the candidates looked more competent. There weren't any instructions about what 'competent' should mean – the participants had to make their own judgements. The researchers found that people tended to agree about which faces looked more competent. That in itself should give us pause – if most people agree on whether a person is competent, does that mean they are right, and one person really is more competent, or is there something else going on?

But, those questions aside, that's not the only thing the study showed – it turned out that those identified as having a more competent face were also more likely to have actually won an election.

We might think this was just a random quirk of one election or one study, but it's a finding that has been replicated time and time again.[3,4,5] It seems that viewing someone's face for less than a second is enough for people to make a rating of their 'competence' that predicts who will win an election. The predictions aren't entirely accurate obviously, but they are still reliable – they can range from 55 to 70 per cent for different elections.

This would seem to suggest that people are generally agreed upon who looks more competent – and that the favoured candidate tends to win elections. Just from a split-second glimpse at a photograph – it's nothing to do with what they say, or what kinds of policies they promote.

And it's not just that participants are aware of who has won a particular election, and (consciously or otherwise) view successful politicians as more competent. For example, in one study people in the USA were able to correctly guess the winner of elections in Bulgaria.[6] Those in the USA and India were also able to correctly guess electoral success in Mexico and Brazil. Interestingly, this study indicated that the effect might be weaker for incumbent candidates – so when voters know how a candidate has actually performed in office, they're less influenced by how that candidate looks.[7]

This effect does vary across cultures, though. There is some evidence showing that perceived 'competence' is more likely to win you an election in the USA than in some other countries, for example South Korea.[8] And it isn't always possible to predict results in another country. For example, while Japanese and American participants were able to guess who won elections in their own countries, they were less successful when judging the politicians from the other country.[9] In the USA success seemed to be better predicted by how 'powerful' the candidate looked, whereas in Japan perceived 'warmth' was more important.

If there are 'social norms' that influence how we perceive leadership in faces across cultures, it seems that we start to pick up on these very early on in life. In a wonderfully titled paper in *Science* ('Predicting Elections: Child's Play'),[10] two researchers called John Antonakis and Olaf Dalgas from the University of Lausanne found that even children are able to make judgements that can predict who is likely to win an election. Of course, you can't really ask a five-year-old to rate how 'competent' a face is, so Antonakis and Dalgas instead asked, 'Who would you like to be the captain of your boat?' From the age of five (as young as they tested) to seventy, answers to this question consistently predicted who would win a given election. Whatever it is about a person's face that makes us think they are more competent in our culture, kids seem to be aware of this from as young an age as we can test them.

So what does all this tell us about how we vote?

For starters, it seems to suggest that we are agreed on what competence is, and that's what we want in our leaders. If we are all agreed, does that mean we can actually tell how competent a person is? Or are we getting it wrong somehow?

It might not be unreasonable to assume that we're on to something – in fact, sometimes a snap judgement can tell you more than you might think. It brings to mind another bias – the well-documented 'halo effect', which shows that we have a tendency to assume that people who are more attractive are also more intelligent.[11]

While this assumption might seem naive, some studies have shown that there may be a little bit of truth to it – people rated as 'attractive', on average, do tend slightly to be more intelligent. The reasons why are not clear – for example, perhaps attractive students get more attention in school – and, of course, it doesn't mean that attractive people are *always* more intelligent.

This halo effect does seem to influence elections. A study in Finland asked people to rate a number of faces according to their 'beauty' – that is, according to their own personal standards of beauty – and found that those candidates identified as more beautiful received 20 per cent more votes.[12] (Even scientists seem to be hit by this halo effect, with more attractive scientists being rated as more 'interesting', although, oddly, people don't necessarily think that makes them better scientists.)[13]

Does something similar apply to our perceptions of competence? Sadly, no: there is no evidence that people are actually able to judge from someone's face whether they are more competent (or indeed more able to captain a boat). While we might *agree* – for whatever cultural reasons – on which faces we think are most competent, this particular bias seems to be unfounded – we just can't tell with any accuracy.

That's unlucky for all of those competent politicians out there who just happen to have the wrong kind of face. Of course there are many other overriding factors that directly influence how we vote, but there seems to be a small but reliable correlation between how we rate their competence in a snap judgement, and how successful they'll be in an election, and the effect of the Nixon/Kennedy debate certainly would support that.

Strictly speaking, there is so far no incontrovertible evidence showing that this bias *directly* affects the way we vote. As with all correlations (such as between ice cream sales and the number of people who drown on a given day), we have to be very careful before saying that one thing really *causes* the other. Actually demonstrating it would be extremely difficult. The only way we could test it with certainty would be for a political party to run a controlled experiment in which they selected equally matched politicians who differed in nothing other than the perceived competence of their faces, and it's unlikely any party would want to take part in such a study. Caveats aside, though, it's certainly striking enough to make us pause and question what kind of biases are behind our decisions when we go to the ballot box.

⟨✗⟩

Overall, it's very sensible for politicians to be concerned about the way they look – it clearly matters. They can't necessarily control their faces, but they can control their general appearance.

It goes without saying that many voters will have certain expectations of how politicians present themselves, and their image is often carefully crafted to appeal to their target audience.

But can the way someone dresses – or the way they do their hair – really encourage us to vote for them? It might seem preposterous but, as always, there are interesting psychological studies that can help us to understand what we're seeing in election campaigns and results.

Let's start with what we can tell about a person's politics just from looking at them.

If you were asked to guess whether a politician was left or right wing, just by looking at their face, how accurate do you think you'd be? Surely you can't tell political allegiance based on looks alone? It's highly unlikely that you'd be 100 per cent accurate, but studies have shown that you are indeed more likely to guess correctly than incorrectly.[14]

When I first heard about this finding, I was sceptical. How can we possibly make an accurate snap judgement about something as important as someone's political views, which can take a whole lifetime to develop? So, I set out to replicate this experiment in my own work.

I gathered a collection of portrait photographs of politicians from sixteen different countries (including Canada, the UK and Australia) and showed them to people from various different countries (mainly Belgians, as that's where we were doing the research, but not exclusively). The accuracy was only around 60 per cent – but, with nothing but a picture to go on, and with a spread of different nationalities included, this result is still surprising.

To try to pinpoint the basis on which people were making their judgements, we tried a second experiment to see what would happen if we showed just the 'internal' facial features (eyes, nose and mouth), or if we showed just the 'external' facial features (chin, jawline, hairstyle). We found that people could guess much more accurately when they could see the external features of the face. So even though we still don't know exactly what it is about someone's appearance that allows us to make these judgements, it's likely that a large part of the effect comes from aspects of appearance that people can cultivate, like their hairstyles. (For example, in some cases we might be picking up on a stereotype for a kind of 'right-wing' power hair style – think Margaret Thatcher.)

These are politicians – and their aim is to appeal to voters, so they may well deliberately style themselves to appeal to certain parts of the electorate (though there is evidence that we're able to make reasonably accurate guesses about political views when looking at members of the public too).

These snap judgements also seem to influence the way we vote, beyond the obvious fact that we're voting for either left- or right-wing candidates. Even the smallest differences in appearance can have an effect.

A study by researchers in the USA showed that looking more 'Republican' could win you more votes in Republican states.[15] Analysing the data from past elections, they discovered that a Republican candidate in one state who looks the part will win more votes, on average, than a Republican candidate in another state who looks less 'Republican'. It's also been shown that Democrats can get more votes in Republican states by looking more 'Republican'.

In contrast, however, politicians who looked more like Democrats didn't seem to do any better in more Democratic states. So this bias – if we can call it a bias – seems to hold more for Republican voters. This might make some sense in the context of some of the findings we discussed in Chapters 1 and 2.

As we have seen, right-wing voters often value group loyalty and respect to authority, they are more likely to endorse traditional values and they tend overall to be more conscientious. It's clearly important for right-wing politicians to signal their support for traditional values and respect for conventions in the way they look, and this can contribute to their success with certain voters, especially those who are more protective of the status quo.

This was memorably demonstrated in one of the most famous exchanges between then-Prime Minister David Cameron and Leader of the Opposition Jeremy Corbyn, in which Cameron offered Corbyn some gentle advice to 'put on a proper suit and do up your tie'. There could be no more direct illustration of someone on the right admonishing someone on the left for not living up to the expected customs and conventions of political office. Over his career Corbyn had made a point of defending his right to wear rustic jumpers in the House of Commons (at one time saying, 'It's not a private members' club.'). However, since taking up a position of more importance on the national stage, Corbyn seems to have followed Cameron's advice, and in the 2017 election campaign he almost always appeared in a smart shirt.

Although such concerns clearly don't come naturally to Corbyn, over time he seems to have decided to respect other people's expectations, and he was probably right to do so if he wanted to broaden his appeal among the voting public.

Of course not all politicians of the left will challenge the status quo quite so directly. Most politicians will attempt to appeal across the political spectrum – and of course they will be trying to look as competent as possible.

Being caught in a compromising position is potentially disastrous and politicians are well aware of this. In the run-up to the 2015 election, for example, some parts of the right-wing British press were very effective in publicising a particularly embarrassing photo of the left-wing candidate for prime minister, Ed Miliband, eating a bacon sandwich. Of course this made for a handy pun ('save our bacon'), but campaign advisors for the Conservative Party were likely very conscious of the influence such an image might have. When she was running in the primaries to be nominated as the Democratic candidate, Hillary Clinton told Stephen Colbert that was exactly why she didn't eat in front of the press: 'They could get a funny shot. You know, something could drop out of your mouth. You could smear your face . . . anything that makes you look silly.'

Politicians are always ready to pounce on something that could undermine their opponents in this way. When footage emerged showing Hillary Clinton stumbling as she got into a car, Donald Trump ran attack ads accusing her of lacking the 'fortitude, strength or stamina' to lead the country. Meanwhile, Obama's White House spokesman Josh Earnest said that Trump's appearance

– and particularly his hair – made it easy to understand why people didn't regard him as a serious candidate: 'The Trump campaign has had a dustbin of history-like quality to it, from the vacuous sloganeering, to the outright lies to even the fake hair, the whole carnival barker routine,' he said.

Does Trump's hairstyle really say anything about his character or candidacy? Does Hillary Clinton's stumble really say anything about her stamina? Probably not. So, is the influence of someone's appearance on how we vote a 'bias'? Well, yes and no. As we've seen, a bias sometimes implies a deviation from what is objectively correct – our perceptions or beliefs don't match the facts.

If we really do vote for people who we think look more competent, that clearly is a bias, as there is no evidence that we can accurately guess whether someone will make for a more competent politician just from looking at their face.

However, if someone is 'biased' to vote for candidates who look conventional in their appearance (or, indeed, unconventional), who is to say whether that is a bias? If voters want candidates who meet their expectations of how they think politicians should appear, that isn't objectively incorrect.

And, of course, we are all different. From conversations I've had with voters over the years, it is clear that some people really focus on the policies of the party they support, while others put much more emphasis on the 'leadership' qualities of the candidates. And, as Nixon found out, sometimes appearance really does count.

5

MAKING THE HEADLINES

In Oscar Wilde's 1890 novel *The Picture of Dorian Gray*, Lord Henry Wotton utters the famous line: 'There is only one thing in the world worse than being talked about, and that is not being talked about.'

I suspect Donald Trump would agree; there can be few politicians who have ever taken such a single-minded approach to the cultivation of fame.

When he announced his intention to run for president in 2015 it was on a stage in the basement of his Trump Tower building in Manhattan, in front of eight American flags.

'Sadly the American dream is dead, but if I get elected president I will bring it back,' he said, before turning his wrath on Mexico, which he accused of 'bringing their worst people', including criminals and 'rapists' to America, accusing China of taking 'our jobs', threatening to be 'tough' on ISIS and insulting fellow Republican candidate Jeb Bush – 'How the hell can you vote for this guy?' – guaranteeing that he led the news on all media outlets.

Widely dismissed – including by notable Republicans and conservatives – in favour of the more 'serious' or conventional candidates, his attention-grabbing comments about building a wall along the US–Mexico border, banning Muslims from the USA and so on, were widely pilloried in the media, but did nothing to halt his ascendancy.

Each new tweet, no matter how absurd, ill conceived or false (a PolitiFact study found that only 5 per cent of the claims Trump made during the 2016 campaign were wholly true and that 69 per cent were either mostly false, false or 'pants on fire'), was widely reported on, even if only to be mocked.

As his campaign gathered momentum, and his leadership opponents fell by the wayside, most of those in Trump's own party maintained distance from him, continuing to comment negatively on his outbursts. And, right up to the day of the election, most of the US (and world) media were united in their condemnation of this most unusual of candidates.

However, despite all this negative coverage, Trump was elected president.

Through it all Trump has consistently accused the media of bias. And he's right, of course.

All media are biased in some way or another – implicitly or explicitly. Whatever your opinion, you can probably find a news source that will confirm your own beliefs (as we saw in Chapter 4), and 'media bias' is a fairly well-established phenomenon. And, it goes without saying that politicians and their spin doctors who try to shape the news cycle are inherently biased. In tandem with (or in opposition to) the media, they work hard to present their own versions of the world, and make their preferred facts and figures stick in the public's mind.

Some news sources at least strive for impartiality. The BBC's Charter and Agreement requires the corporation to be impartial and it trains its reporters, via its academy, to recognise their own bias: 'Impartiality can mean challenging your own assumptions or those of your team or contributors.' Similarly, Reuters has a policy of taking a 'value-neutral approach', and its editorial policy states: 'We are committed to reporting the facts and in all situations avoid the use of emotive terms.'

However, most of the media is openly partial, explicitly endorsing certain parties or candidates or points of view. Trump's objection to partisan news almost certainly wasn't based on principle. It was just disappointing to Trump that, apart from outliers such as TV pundit Sean Hannity and right-wing website Breitbart News, most of the media, including most conservative media, didn't endorse him – he objected to that particular 'bias'.

But rather than focusing on Trump and how the media might be partial or 'biased', I'd like to focus on what goes on in our own heads that makes us resistant or receptive to what the media has to say. What cognitive biases come into play and do how they affect what we make of the media?

Media coverage certainly affects how we vote, but not necessarily in the way you might expect. Exploring the nature of this influence can help us to understand some of the ways in which we form our political priorities and decide what we think is true. And it can reveal how subtle changes in the way an issue is framed in the media can shape our interpretation of it.

$$\boxed{X}$$

Some parts of the media make quite bold claims about the effect they have on our political decisions. In the UK the *Sun* newspaper, for example, always endorses a candidate in a general election and this used to be considered a very powerful message to the electorate. Following the 1992 election they ran with the headline 'It's The Sun Wot Won It'. Hillary Clinton racked up at least 186 endorsements running against Trump – including publications with a solid record of endorsing Republicans such as the *Dallas Morning News* and *Columbus Dispatch*, as well as the *San Diego Union-Tribune* and *Arizona Republic*, neither of which had endorsed a Democrat for over a century. And in Australia, concern about media influence led to the passing of a law in 1992 banning all election TV advertising from midnight on the Wednesday before polling day to the close of polls on polling day – always a Saturday – to allow voters a 'cooling off' period to consider the issues.

So, is the media good at telling us what to think?

In the USA, there had been so much propaganda during the Second World War to promote the war effort and national security that, after the conflict had ended, researchers started studying the effects of the mass media. They were keen to know if the propaganda was changing people's perceptions, and creating a passive, easily manipulated public.

Unexpectedly, the answer was no – people weren't easily being 'led astray'; in fact, the propaganda had done little to change people's minds; it only managed to reinforce their views if they already agreed.[1]

Humans can be a stubborn lot – for better or for worse we have a number of biases that can make us resistant to persuasion. As we saw in Chapter 4, our minds have some strategies for making us think we're right – it can be hard for us to see the other side's perspective, and we'll tend to focus on evidence that reinforces our own point of view. Our psychology can make us stand firm when we've already made up our minds, especially in areas where we have a lot of knowledge or already have strong opinions. Crucially, though, that doesn't just apply to propaganda. Even when the media is making us aware of facts backed up by science, which we'll look at in Chapter 6, we can be less susceptible to the message, especially if it contradicts our deeply held beliefs and values.

In a way, those mid-century Americans were protected from propaganda by their biases. Although perhaps they also didn't quite trust the sources of propaganda. Curiously, a study published in 2011 suggested that political endorsements that diverge from the publication's normal stance – say, a conservative newspaper supporting a Democrat – have a greater impact on readers' choices.[2] Voters' trust increases when they perceive a lower degree of bias, and they perceive less bias when an outlet defies its own conventions.

The media isn't an all-powerful propaganda machine – as we've seen in the case of Trump, who was elected despite the media being widely against him. It isn't necessarily successful in telling us exactly *what* to think – but we can be open to persuasion in other ways.

☒

When you think about the issues that are most pressing in the world today, what comes to mind? Depending on who and where you are, they might include climate change, big banking, defence and security, immigration, women's rights or poverty.

Why might you focus on particular topics like these? Why do they seem more important to you than other issues at this moment in time?

When you see a story about one of these subjects, you're likely to be drawn to it. But perhaps you're interested partly *because* you've seen so many stories in the media already.

In 1922 the American journalist Walter Lippmann wrote the influential book *Public Opinion*. In those early days of the mass media – newspapers, radio and filmed newsreels – he took a dim view of their ability to inform the public, famously writing that the press was 'like the beam of a searchlight that moves restlessly about, bringing one episode and then another out of the darkness into vision'.

By selecting one issue rather than another, the media focuses our attention. It is setting the agenda, defining people's priorities – the things they think are most important in the world right now. As the American political scientist Bernard Cohen claimed in 1963: 'While the press may not be successful much of the time in telling people what to think, it is stunningly successful in telling its readers what to think about.'[3]

In 1982 a famous study by scientists at Yale University and the University of Michigan set out to discover just how much direct influence the media can have on our political priorities.

Shanto Iyengar, Mark D. Peters and Donald R. Kinder recruited a group of people and asked them which of the prominent topics of the day they most cared about, ranked in order of importance.[4] They then split them into two groups: the 'experimental' group and the 'control' group. Over some days, the experimental group watched the news every evening, but the broadcast had been manipulated to focus more on defence issues. The control group watched undoctored news reports.

After a few evenings of watching this doctored news, participants were questioned on their views again, and the effects were clear. When first asked, the experimental group had ranked defence sixth out of eight problems (following inflation, pollution, unemployment, energy and civil rights). After watching the news, defence had leapt up to second place, with inflation remaining in first place. For those who saw the ordinary reports, the ranking of defence stayed the same.

In a second experiment, the researchers set out to explore whether people could be influenced by three different topics. One group watched news with extra defence stories, another group watched news with more on inflation, and another saw more on pollution. The results were largely as expected: participants with more defence-related news increased their rating of the importance of defence, and those exposed to more pollution-related stories increased their rating of the importance of pollution. The 'extra inflation news' participants also rated inflation as more important than the other groups, but the increase wasn't significant (though that might have been because they already thought inflation was very important at the start of the experiment).

Crucially, though, the way in which the news was doctored also influenced how participants viewed the US president in 1981, Jimmy Carter. The researchers asked people in both experiments how they rated President Carter on the subjects they'd been primed on. If the respondents had seen the doctored news stories they were more likely to be concerned about his performance in those areas. And that led them to be more concerned when evaluating Carter's overall performance as well.

The evidence was clear: if a problem was prominently featured in the TV news, it became a much more important factor in how people judged the president's performance.

X

Stories in the news affect our priorities and how we see the political world around us, and often we don't even realise we're being influenced. But it's not simply because we're just passively absorbing whatever information is presented to us.

It's partly a result of the mind's active attempt to make the best use of whatever information is most *available* to it.

The human brain is more powerful than any computer. Sometimes, however, when faced with extremely complex decisions, rather than fully weigh up all the options, it employs some mental shortcuts. Those decision-making shortcuts – sometimes known as 'heuristics' – can influence our judgements of what is important. In this case, we are biased by something called the 'availability heuristic'.

This mental shortcut is one of the many heuristics and psychological tendencies made famous by the

Nobel Prize-winning psychologist and behavioural economist Daniel Kahneman and his colleague Amos Tversky (their remarkable relationship was the subject of a book called *The Undoing Project* by bestselling author Michael Lewis). Wondering whether people really were the rational decision-makers they were believed to be (at least by economists), in the 1960s and 1970s they started investigating some of the mental shortcuts we use when we're operating in uncertain conditions. In 1973 they published a seminal paper in which they identified this availability heuristic.[5]

The idea is that if something can be remembered or brought to mind easily, it becomes more important or relevant to us, and that affects our judgements.

Here's a simple example.

Try to bring to mind one or two positive things that happened to you last week. They could be anything – a special family moment, a success at work, a fun night out with friends.

Now answer the question: 'How happy were you last week?'

What will you base your answer on? It's likely that it will be influenced by whatever memories are most easily available to you. In this case, if you've been thinking of positive things that happened to you, you're more likely to say you were happier.

Obviously if you've had an exceptionally good (or bad) week, then thinking of a couple of things might not have a huge effect; but for an average week about which you don't yet have a strong opinion, your mind will bias its answer based on the positive (or, conversely, negative) events you've just been thinking about, simply because they come more easily to mind.

There are many ways this bias can affect our judgement. If you have a lot of friends who've had heart attacks, you're likely to think that heart attacks are more common than they actually are. Or, in business, people think an investment is better or worse depending on what they've recently seen about that company, rather than looking at all the facts.

If something comes to mind more easily, it might be because you've seen it a few times, or because it was particularly dramatic or vivid (or emotionally wrenching – as many news items are), or perhaps you came across it particularly recently.

This means that, when thinking about big issues (or evaluating a president, as in the experiment with Carter mentioned above), we're more likely to bring to mind recent examples from the news, rather than examining all the alternative sources of information – and those recent examples are likely to have a disproportionate influence on our judgements.

What really makes the difference here, according to other research, is the *ease* of recall.

In 2002 a British team set out to test this with a real-world example: they decided to find out how people perceived the then British prime minister, Tony Blair.[6] They asked a number of people who weren't very politically engaged to think back and list a specific number of positive things (either two or five) about Blair, or the same number of negative things. And then they asked the respondents their attitude towards him. Surprisingly, what affected the answers to this question wasn't whether the respondents had been asked to think of positive things or negative things – it was whether they had found it easy to recall those positive or negative points in the first place.

If people had struggled to come up with a lot of negative things to say about Blair, that made them like him *more* than the people who'd listed positive attributes – presumably because, if they couldn't quickly think of something bad to say, then he couldn't be that bad. They were basing their judgements of him on how easily these things came to mind, not on any further research, analysis or reflection.

Like most cognitive biases, the availability heuristic certainly has its uses. If you're asked to name the capital of a foreign country and you're not sure of the answer, going with whatever city first comes to mind is probably a decent strategy. But when making a complex decision that relies on an understanding of how the world works this bias can lead us astray.

The influential psychologist and linguist Steven Pinker made this point in his book *The Better Angels of Our Nature*. Pinker points out that the media frequently show us examples of conflicts, war zones and famine: those are the stories that they consider important, that they think we want or need to know about, and that is not necessarily a bad thing.

But the result is that people often think the level of war and violent death in the world is as high as ever (or even worse than it was in the past), when actually the number of violent deaths per head of population is at an all-time low. We often assume that global poverty is at an all-time high too – but, again, as a proportion of the world's population the number of people living in poverty has dramatically reduced during the last fifty years.

Most of us don't have a broader understanding of the statistical trends, and so, when we think about the state of the world, the examples depicted in the media are the ones that come most easily to mind, and we use them to make our judgements.

And don't forget – the media and politicians can make use of this by pushing the political agenda onto issues that are naturally the territory of one party or another. The right is usually stronger on issues of defence, crime and law and order, for example, so in an election cycle news stories that emphasise those events naturally play to the right. The left is usually stronger on issues such as inequality and minority rights, so stories that emphasise exploitation or discrimination will naturally benefit the left.[7]

Trump's 2016 campaign functioned like no other to control the news agenda. With a single provocative tweet, he could put his issues, his name and his brand at the top of the news cycle. The coverage was as widespread as it was negative. And it was certainly negative. One estimate suggested that of all the times Trump was mentioned in the media, 96 per cent of the articles expressed a negative opinion.

However, Trump focused on making some simple, memorable messages available. Build a wall. Bring jobs back to America. 'Crooked Hillary'. 'Make America great again'. And a large portion of the US electorate was not influenced by the media's negative coverage – they weren't told *what* to think – but they certainly felt they knew what was important, what everyone was talking about . . . and that was Trump.

☒

Trump knew that media exposure, even negative exposure, could be a gift to his campaign. Perhaps he is familiar with what psychologists call the 'mere exposure effect'.

The idea here is that when something – or someone – is more familiar to us, we like it more (hence some psychologists regard it as part of a broader 'familiarity bias').

When we're repeatedly exposed to something, its familiarity means we are more likely to be welcoming of it.

The Polish-American social psychologist Robert Zajonc first coined the term 'mere exposure effect' in 1968. He opened his paper with this intriguing example:[8]

'On February 27, 1967, the Associated Press carried the following story from Corvallis, Oregon: "A mysterious student has been attending a class at Oregon State University for the past two months enveloped in a big black bag. Only his bare feet show. Each Monday, Wednesday and Friday at 11.00 a.m. the Black Bag sits on a small table near the back of the classroom. The class is Speech 113 – basic persuasion ... Charles Goetzinger, professor of the class, knows the identity of the person inside. None of the 20 students in the class do. Goetzinger said *the students' attitude changed from hostility toward the Black Bag to curiosity and finally to friendship* [italics added]."'

Zajonc went on to test the effect in a range of ways, showing that, on average, if we see a random arrangement of letters a number of times ('ryiane', for example), we will start to prefer it to other orders that we are not familiar with. So just by exposing a person to something, you can improve their attitude towards it (hence 'mere' exposure).

There have since been a huge number of studies showing how this effect can influence us in a wide range of situations. For example, you are more likely to be well disposed to someone you occasionally see in the street than someone you've never seen before. It might be because you haven't had a reason to be frightened of that person, so every time you see them, that lack of threat is reinforced, even though you don't actually know anything about them. It is a strange but reliable effect, and often we don't even realise that it is happening. We don't think we prefer things because we've seen them before – we like them more because, well, we just do.

A lot of advertising is effective for this reason – the overt message of the ad might not filter through, but just being exposed to the brand name makes the product more familiar, and more appealing, when we next see it.

The same effect also comes into play in politics. An American study showed that seeing a candidate more often – their media exposure – can affect their success in the polls by 5–10 per cent.[9]

So, the more we see something in the media, the more familiar it can seem to us and the more positive we feel about it – which means that just the repeated coverage of an idea or candidate in the media can be helpful over time. But this well-documented bias has another side, too.

Surprisingly, it also applies to whether we think things are *true*.[10]

In a simple experiment in the 1970s, three American psychologists called Lynn Hasher, David Goldstein and Thomas Toppino wanted to find out if this 'familiarity effect' extended not just to whether we liked something but also to whether we thought it was true or false. If you hear something often enough, do you start to believe it?

Take the statement: 'The total population of Greenland is about 50,000.' It sounds plausible enough, though most of us won't know if it's really true or not without checking. In the absence of certainty, how do we decide?

Hasher and her colleagues had a suspicion: the more often you hear that Greenland has 50,000 inhabitants, the more likely you are to think it's true. And they were right.

In their experiment they asked people to rate whether they thought sixty statements (on politics, sports and the arts) were true or false. They ran three sessions, two weeks apart, and a small number of the statements were repeated across the sessions. What they found is that, with repetition, people were more and more likely to rate the repeated statements as true, whether or not the statements were in fact true (e.g. 'Total U.S. defence spending has risen steadily since 1965') or false (e.g. 'The People's Republic of China was founded in 1947').

You might get a feel for this effect if you remember the research about monkeys from Chapter 1: the study showing that monkeys are normally happy to perform a task for a piece of celery, but will protest when they see another monkey being rewarded with grapes for the same task.

Does that research feel more familiar this time? Does that familiarity somehow feel reassuring? Perhaps you even feel more confident that it's true?

I haven't provided you with any more evidence that it's true; I've simply repeated it.

In politics, this effect is only likely to have an influence in areas where voters know little about the issues or candidates, but in terms of the actual facts, that probably covers a lot of modern-day politics for most of us (something we will explore further in Chapter 8).

That's why successful political campaigns focus on key 'sound-bite' figures. They can make sure these figures reach audiences via media outlets that are looking for easy material, and their repeated exposure makes them somehow more believable over time. US president Ronald Reagan's ability to connect with voters earned him the nickname the 'Great Communicator', and his ability was greatly enhanced by his – or at least his team's – understanding of how the news cycle operated, which they then kept fed with short, memorable phrases such as: 'Government is not the solution to our problem; government is the problem' and 'Mr Gorbachev, tear down this wall!'

In the run-up to the EU referendum, the Leave campaign stated as regularly and often as it could the claim that the UK sent £350 million a week to the EU – a figure which they even emblazoned across their battle bus. The UK Statistics Authority said this figure was not just potentially misleading, but misleading plain and simple, and the respected Institute for Fiscal Studies called it 'absurd'. But each time the Remain campaign challenged the figure of £350 million, it probably ended up reinforcing the memory of the figure in people's minds. A simple number was easier to remember than any of the critical arguments (a lot of that money returns directly in the form of subsidies and investment, and the broader benefits of membership of the single market are hard to quantify), so the debate became anchored to that number.

In the US election of 2016, with the repetition of 'lock her up' at Trump rallies, and the constant coverage of his claims about Clinton's supposed malfeasance, the idea of 'crooked Hillary' was more likely to seem true with every repetition. Of course we now know that Trump had no intention of locking her up, and said in the days after the election it was 'no longer something he felt so strongly about' and that he did not want to 'hurt the family'.

Knowing about your own inbuilt tendency to believe and trust things that you've seen before, and to build arguments based on things you can most easily remember, might cause you to pause the next time you get into a heated political debate.

Most psychologists are fairly pessimistic about our ability to counteract these biases. But it can make for an interesting exercise to question some of the facts and figures or arguments that are so familiar we usually accept them without challenge. Are they as valid as you've always assumed? As we'll see in the next chapter, sometimes when an incorrect notion gets lodged in our minds (Did Iraq have weapons of mass destruction? Can vaccines cause Autism?) it can prove very hard to change.

✗

When Trump said he wanted to ban all Muslims from the USA and build a wall along the US–Mexico border, he presented these policies as national security issues. His opponents presented them in terms of racism and human rights.

Similarly, when Angela Merkel opened up Germany's borders, she talked about the measure as a compassionate decision on her part, calling it 'our humanitarian duty'. For her opponents, it was a dilution of German culture and a risk to public safety; and she was particularly criticised for the policy in the wake of the Berlin attack, when a truck was driven into crowds at the Christmas markets. The attack, carried out by an asylum seeker, left twelve people dead.

When it comes to decisions on issues such as human rights or public safety, the facts might be simple, but their interpretation rarely is. In 1981, in a hugely influential article called 'Framing Decisions and the Psychology of Choice', Kahneman and Tversky outlined yet another way in which the decisions we make are not always as rational as we think they are.[11] How we perceive or make choices on a particular issue depends on how that choice is 'framed'.

They tested their idea by presenting people with a choice that potentially had a life or death outcome. In the case of an epidemic, they had to choose between two

options for a vaccine trial – both had a chance of resulting in some deaths, as well as a chance of saving lives.

The two available options remained the same
throughout the experiment but the researchers varied
the way they were framed, sometimes emphasising the
positives or negatives (lives saved or lost) of one option
and sometimes of the other. What they found was that
these variations of framing could dramatically affect the
number of people who would choose either option (most
would go for the positive framing).

Since their pioneering work, this phenomenon has
been investigated widely around the world. It's a subject of particular relevance to politics. After all, the art
of political spin is, to a large extent, a question of how
news stories are framed, and there's one very famous
study that demonstrates how it can affect our political
judgements.[12]

In 1997 researchers in the USA created two different news reports about a Ku Klux Klan rally, and showed
them to two separate groups of people.

The first version framed the KKK rally as a free
speech issue. The article included protestors' signs saying
'No free speech for racists', quotes from supporters saying they should be able to hear if they want to, and some
photographs of protestors and leaders speaking at the
microphone. We might imagine a TV voiceover to read

something along the lines of: 'In a key test of the limits of free speech today the Ku Klux Klan made a controversial speech ...'

The second version framed the rally as a public order issue. This article quoted observers and reporters seeing 'real sparks in the crowd' and the 'tension between Klan protestors and supporters came within seconds of violence', alongside photos of police officers protecting Klan members from the protestors. For this version, we might imagine a TV voiceover to be: 'There was tension in the centre of the city today as members of the Ku Klux Klan made a controversial speech ...'

Seeing one article or the other could make a big difference to the way people judged the event, but it also went on to affect their general attitudes to the KKK. When the rally was presented as a free speech issue, people were much more likely to express tolerance of such rallies and speeches.

Our tendency to interpret events and information according to how they're 'framed' is very powerful. This is partly because in framing issues it's possible to stress specific values or beliefs that we might hold very deeply.

As we mentioned earlier, sometimes when the things we read conflict with our deeply held values that makes us more likely to resist them.

But the opposite is also true – if something is presented as being in line with those beliefs, we can be more open to interpreting the facts in a particular way.

The media inevitably have to make choices about how to frame a story. To take a less emotive contemporary example, imagine a news report running one headline: 'Traffic was massively disrupted today as environmental protestors blockaded a road outside an airport to oppose expansion', or another: 'To make a stand on the environmental impact of a new runway environmental protestors blockaded a road outside an airport today'. Both versions could be completely true, but whether the story is framed in terms of the disruption to traffic or as an environmental stand is likely to influence our opinion of it.

For any media wishing to offer a truly impartial version of events, this presents a challenging dilemma. How a journalist chooses to tell a story may reflect their own interpretation – and that could be a conscious decision, or not.

For those of us who consume the media, our own values, and how they complement or conflict with the framing of a story, will shape what we think of the 'facts'. Think about that the next time you read a news story; if it had been framed in a different way, would you have interpreted those facts differently?

✗

How we perceive and interpret political issues and events is influenced by the media in certain ways that might not be obvious at first. The media's priorities shape our priorities; whether or not we notice changes in immigration in our local area might depend upon how salient the media has made that issue. When faced with complex, uncertain decisions, our minds will naturally look to whatever facts or stories are most available; and how those facts have been framed can change how we interpret them. The ease with which we can then recall those facts, and how familiar they feel to us, can also shape our perceptions and arguments.

So even though for most of us the media coverage of an election can't directly change our vote, it can still certainly have an influence on our views and perceptions, upon which our vote ultimately depends. That may not sound overly alarming; perhaps you trust your news sources to provide you with what you judge as relevant and important information. But with the rise of fake news spreading false stories around the internet, perhaps we do need to be more aware of the subtle ways in which we can be swayed by the media.

6

FAKING IT

In 2016 the issue of fake news exploded onto the political landscape during the US presidential election. Across the internet people were discussing and sharing stories of wildly varying degrees of improbability: 'Clinton sold weapons to Isis'; 'Trump endorsed by Pope'.

At one point during the election campaign, an analysis from Buzzfeed suggested that these fake news stories were getting more attention on Facebook than real ones.

But fake news isn't a new phenomenon.

Robert Parkinson, a professor at Binghamton University, pointed out in the *Washington Post* that while Founding Father Benjamin Franklin was the

American ambassador to France, he created a fake issue of a real Boston newspaper – the *Independent Chronicle* – that included the discovery of bags of 700 human scalps allegedly taken by Indians in league with King George III. Likewise, historian Tim Stanley noted that during the hotly contested 1828 US election (considered by many as the dirtiest election ever) Andrew Jackson started a rumour that John Quincy Adams had bought an American girl in order to satisfy the Tsar of Russia, while Adams spread rumours that Jackson's mother slept with slaves and even had a child with one.

However, while there are historical examples of fake news stories, the rise in cable TV – especially twenty-four-hour rolling news with its increasingly fast-paced cycle – and the power of social networks to spread news farther and faster has made it easier and quicker to reach a much wider audience. Realistic-looking fake news sites have sprung up, spreading misinformation across the globe, whether for a joke, for money, to discredit rival agendas or to promote their own.

After the US election many people claimed that fake news had had a real impact on the outcome of the election, essentially winning it for Trump. Russia, in particular, has been accused of attempting to interfere in the election process, partly because much of the fake news content appears to have originated there.

But can fake news really influence us that easily? Some of the stories were pretty wild and outlandish – it seems implausible that they could have held enough sway to affect the way people voted.

It's hard to say what the actual effect was; just because someone has reacted on Facebook doesn't mean that they'll necessarily have engaged with the content. In fact, in the face of criticism that Facebook should have done more to control the spread of fake news stories, Mark Zuckerburg said it was ridiculous to suggest that it could have influenced the election.

Whether or not that's true, there are certainly examples of people buying into these stories, no matter how bizarre they may sound to some.

One story that did the rounds was of a paedophile ring led by Hillary Clinton operating out of a pizza restaurant in Washington, a story that led to a 'concerned citizen' driving out to the pizzeria, armed with a gun, to investigate the situation for himself. During the incident a weapon was discharged, although no one was injured. That is of course an extreme example, but it nevertheless shows that some people are taken in by these claims.

A less serious, somewhat amusing example was a widely shared meme that claimed Trump, in a 1998 *People* magazine interview, had said, 'If I were to run, I'd run as a Republican. They're the dumbest group of voters in the country. They believe anything on Fox News. I could lie and they'd still eat it up. I bet my numbers would be terrific.' The quote was a lie; Trump never said that. But then, having made so many shocking-but-true statements ('I could stand in the middle of Fifth Avenue and shoot somebody, and I wouldn't lose any voters', for example, is a real one), it can be hard to judge.

There are also ways to make the fabrications sound more believable. Often they mix fact with fiction, opening with a genuine story that then leads into the fake claims. For example, one article quoted various real statements made on abortion by Trump's running mate Mike Pence, but then inserted an entirely fictitious quote on the topic of allowing abortions for rape victims: 'We'd then have an epidemic of women claiming to have been raped just so they could have an abortion.'

Readers who were familiar with Pence's anti-abortion stance, and whose confirmation bias perhaps predisposed them to believe negative things about him, may have felt this had a ring of truth to it, even though it sounds, on its own, rather far-fetched.

Tactics like this are worrying, as is the way that these stories spread. As noted, the internet and social media mean that fake news can reach a wider audience than ever before. And evidence is also emerging that large organisations might be paying for false social media accounts to spread fake news. 'Astroturfing', the practice of hiding the sponsors of a political, advertising, religious or any other kind of message to make it appear as though it originates from ordinary folk (creating 'fake grassroots'), and 'sockpuppetry', the deliberate creation of false online identities to promote opinions – including fake news – have been rampant for years.

Social media is a highly unregulated space, open to exploitation by those with the money to do so. That is one reason why many people are calling for stricter regulation, such as taking greater steps to ensure that all registered users are actually who they claim to be.

Given the ease with which fake news can now spread we are clearly going to have to do more to understand what makes people more susceptible, or resistant, to it.

A paper in *Psychological Science* by Daniel Fessler has shown our receptivity depends on our psychological profile and the nature of the information we receive.[1] It starts out with the following story: 'In 2012, a liberal professor wrote that the Obama Administration was stockpiling ammunition, preparing for totalitarian rule. This idea was ignored by liberals. In 2015, conservative bloggers asserted that a military exercise aimed to occupy Texas and impose martial law. Conservatives became so concerned that the Texas Governor ordered the State Guard to monitor the exercise.'

There are obviously lots of reasons why these conspiracy theories might have been ignored by liberals and raised concerns among some conservatives (not least the differences in their opinions towards Obama), but Fessler and his colleagues suggested that conservatives might be more likely to believe stories that involve potential threats or hazards more generally. In order to test this, they had to invent stories which had no obvious political association, and then test whether conservatives were more likely to believe the statements that implied certain hazards.

That is exactly what they found.

Conservatives were much more likely to say they believed 'Kale 156 contains thallium, a toxic heavy metal, that the plant absorbs from soil', for example, than 'Eating carrots results in significantly improved vision'. This reaction fits with the personality traits we saw in Chapter 2, with those on the right being somewhat more sensitive to threats.

As far as I know, there aren't any studies showing that liberals are more receptive to certain claims or other forms of fake news. Before liberals take this as a win for their side however, it's worth highlighting that most of the professors conducting this kind of research are themselves liberals. As objectively as they try to approach their research this will probably bias their focus. If there were more conservative professors in social psychology, I suspect there would be more research articles about the sort of fake news to which liberals are more susceptible.

One thing is certain: fake news is big news for modern democracies.

$$\boxed{\textit{X}}$$

There are plenty of dubious and misleading news stories out there, and the likelihood is that at some point we will accidentally get taken in by one; but whether we do or not, we are perhaps becoming increasingly distrustful of the stories and 'facts' we come across everywhere. And that poses a problem: in order to make informed and rational decisions, we have to have sources we can trust – including so-called 'experts'.

In the run-up to the EU referendum in the UK, Vote Leave campaigner Michael Gove dismissed some of the financial predictions of the economic consequences of Brexit, stating boldly 'people in this country have had enough of experts'. Is he right?

We all have to rely on experts of one form or another at different times in our lives. Almost by definition, because they have expertise that we don't, our reliance on them demands a certain degree of trust. When it comes to something like fixing our boiler, in most cases we can feel confident that our trust has been well placed in a trained professional – or at least it will become obvious fairly quickly if it was not.

But when it comes to something as complex as deciding whether to leave the EU, on what basis can we decide which experts to rely on, when there are so many conflicting opinions and 'facts' being touted around?

Indeed, as we saw in Chapter 4, it's apparent from Philip Tetlock's work that many of these 'experts' are unable to make accurate predictions (though they still seemed to convince themselves that they could). That particular study included a lot of so-called TV pundits, but the problem is widespread and we are all susceptible to unwittingly relying on the wrong information.

Take for example the story of a young professional named George. Like many people nowadays, George studied for a degree that didn't equip him with much of the expertise he needed in his desired line of work. Luckily, however, there was a wealth of published academic research that helped to guide him.

More specifically, George was working in the field of economics, and trying to understand how levels of public debt (how much a country has borrowed) relate to economic growth. Two Harvard professors, Reinhart and Rogoff, had published some very influential research showing that the higher a country's debt, the lower its level of growth.[2] Perfect. George used this to argue that in order for a country to grow, it had to take big steps to reduce national debt.

Unfortunately for George, however, not long after the study had been published some students at the nearby University of Massachusetts were set the task of replicating Reinhart and Rogoff's results. They couldn't. At first the students assumed they must be making a mistake; eventually they asked if they could have a copy of the data the professors had used, so that they could figure out what they were doing wrong.

It turned out that the error was not with the students, but with the workings of the professors. A few mistakes in an Excel document had skewed the results. Once they had been corrected, the strong relationship between national debt and growth became much less clear.[3] Unfortunately, George had relied on expertise that proved unreliable.

In case it isn't clear already, the George in question was former Chancellor of the Exchequer George Osborne, who cited Reinhart and Rogoff's work as a motivation for his austerity-focused response to the economic crisis. So if politicians can't rely on expert advice to run the country effectively, what hope do the rest of us have?

$\boxed{X}$

Experts are human too and everyone makes mistakes. But sometimes a false finding isn't due to a mistake; rather it's because the study's methods or findings have been intentionally interfered with. Fake news might be grabbing the headlines, but fake science is big news too, and there have been a worrying number of cases in recent years.

In 2011, world-renowned Harvard professor Marc Hauser resigned after an investigation found him guilty of manipulating evidence in a number of studies relating to his work with humans and monkeys, exploring the roots of cognition and morality. Also in 2011 an investigation began into a famous Dutch psychologist, Diederik Stapel (who had, for instance, claimed that meat eaters were more selfish), which concluded that he had manipulated data in as many as fifty-five studies and resulted in the end of his scientific career. And there are instances across all areas of scientific research; an investigation in 2016 by the China Food and Drug Administration (CFDA) into data from 1,622 clinical trials for new pharmaceutical drugs found that 80 per cent of the data failed to meet analysis requirements, were incomplete, or totally non-existent.

In 2015, two graduate students at the University of California, David Broockman and Joshua Kalla, produced evidence that a major paper in *Science* (one of the most prestigious journals in the world) had been faked. The paper claimed to have found evidence that just a few minutes of speaking to a gay political canvasser could influence the opinions of voters who were otherwise opposed to same-sex marriage.

This report was big news, particularly for political science, where it has often proved very difficult to demonstrate that you can ever change people's views (let alone with just a few minutes of canvassing), especially on a highly emotive issue that could make all the difference to how people vote. But when the students tried to understand the methods used in the study, they found various inconsistencies with the paper, eventually leading to *Science* retracting the article.

Although Broockman and Kalla have subsequently shown through their own work that the study's conclusions had merit (as we'll see in Chapter 7), any instance where a study has been shown to be faked or manipulated has a damaging effect, even if the results are later confirmed. It can discredit not just that paper, but potentially other work by the scientist in question, and undermine the trust that we place in the scientific process.

These explicit cases of fraud are probably only a minor issue faced by the scientific community, however.

A much larger problem is what has become known as the 'replication crisis', when other researchers are unable to reproduce the same result for reasons other than manipulated data; the original researchers may simply have found their results by chance. How scientists determine whether they have 'found' a meaningful result is complicated; but suffice to say like the old story about enough monkeys with enough typewriters producing a work of Shakespeare, with enough scientists running enough experiments out there, some of them are bound to accidentally come across significant effects.

In his 2011 book *Thinking, Fast and Slow* Daniel Kahneman reviewed a number of studies in which people were unconsciously primed to behave in particular ways. For example, exposing people to words related to aging seemed to cause them to walk more slowly down the corridor. In the years since the book was published, there have been numerous failures to replicate some of these studies; Kahneman has acknowledged this, and admitted that he probably gave some of these studies too much weight in his writing.

Social psychology in particular has faced a lot of controversy about claims that complex behaviour can be influenced by simple 'priming' effects. Another example particularly important for political psychology claimed to have found evidence that briefly exposing participants to the American flag could make them (both Republican and Democrat) more likely to shift their support towards the Republican party in a number of ways.[4]

Reflecting honestly, had I written this book a few years ago, I might well have included that study as an example of how our vote can be biased. In 2014, however, a systematic attempt to replicate several studies in psychology failed to find evidence for this effect.[5] As an aside, it did demonstrate that a number of the key studies upon which Kahneman built his career replicated very robustly.

This 'replication crisis' has many causes. One of them, as we've seen, is that scientists can sometimes happen upon a finding by chance. This is then compounded by a systematic 'publication bias' in the incentives that shape a scientist's career.

You might hope that science would operate on a purely objective basis when it comes to deciding what studies to publish, but in recent years a culture has developed in which the most interesting or exciting studies are prioritised. Anything not deemed newsworthy, including failures to replicate studies, or studies that don't 'find' something, run the risk of gathering dust in the scientist's 'file drawer'. The focus on objectivity can become a little blurred in the face of demands on scientists to 'publish or perish'.

Even when the science is robust, the media can also sometimes represent studies in a way that was not intended – oversimplifying a finding, perhaps, or taking a result out of context. Just because an interesting development has been noted in the brain of a rat does not necessarily mean some sort of miracle drug is about to transform our lives. And a slight correlation between people who eat a certain food and people who develop cancer doesn't mean that the food causes the cancer.

That hasn't stopped the *Daily Mail* running articles over the years linking cancer to bacon, beef, broccoli, chillies, chips, chocolate, cola, coffee, fruit juice, grapefruit, ham, lamb, milk, mouthwash, peanut butter, pastry, pickles, potatoes, rice, sausages and toast (but only if burnt) – to name but a few. In fact, many of the items it is often claimed can cure or prevent cancer have also been accused of causing cancer, at one time or another.

In 2016, a number of sources reported that a study had shown drinking two to three cups of coffee a day could prevent Alzheimer's – but that was greatly overstating the significance of the results. In fairness to the media however, journalists often have to rely on a university-generated press release when reporting, and a recent study in the *British Medical Journal* found that exaggerated health stories in the news were often associated with exaggerated claims in the press release.[6]

Thankfully there are major developments in progress to restore some of the principles of objectivity to the actual process of science. Ben Goldacre at the University of Oxford has been working to ensure that the results of all medical trials – and the details of who funds them – are made openly available, whatever the outcome. Chris Chambers at the University of Cardiff has been leading an effort for journals in psychology and neuroscience to include an option for 'registered reports' that would accept or reject a study in advance based on the rigour of its design, not the outcome of the data collected. Brian Nosek in the USA has also set up The Center for Open Science, which has been facilitating large-scale attempts to test the robustness and reliability of some areas of science.

Measures like these are important to restore faith in the scientific process. Because, of course, it isn't all wrong! There is plenty we can still rely on. And in some cases it is crucial that the public can be convinced of the reliability of the science, as we'll see with vaccinations and climate change.

$\boxed{x}$

Any instance of fake science is potentially damaging.

When a paper is proved fraudulent, you might hope that it will simply be consigned to history and that the scientific community will dismiss the research and move on. But once fake science gets into the mainstream media, it can prove a lot harder to change people's minds and convince them that the data was wrong.

Perhaps one of the most tragic examples of this was the publication of a link between vaccines and autism in the prestigious medicinal journal the *Lancet*, in 1998. The sample size was just twelve and the first author had an undeclared financial interest in the results of the study. After further scrutiny the journal decided the results didn't actually hold up, and they retracted the paper – it led to investigations of fraud and the lead author was eventually struck off the medical register as a result.

Unfortunately, the story had already been taken up by the popular press, and, despite the fact that there have been multiple studies on the topic since and not one of them has found any link between autism and vaccines, it has proved very hard to correct. There has been a worrying decline in participation in some vaccine programs, which are vital to stop deadly diseases spreading. A measles outbreak in Swansea, between November 2012 and July 2013, resulted in 664 people being infected, eighty-eight being hospitalised and one death. In 2015 two dozen individuals who visited Disneyland in Florida fell ill with measles, and then exported it to three other states: Utah, Colorado and Washington.

One article called the fraudulent report 'the most damaging medical hoax of the last 100 years'.[7] The topic continues to crop up frequently in the news and, according to a 2015 report by the Pew Research Center, about one in ten Americans thinks vaccines are not safe.

There are plenty of other examples of what Stephan Lewandowsky at the University of Bristol calls 'sticky' misinformation. In the run-up to the most recent war in Iraq one of the most prominent arguments for the invasion was that Iraq possessed weapons of mass destruction. Not only have these claims now been refuted, they have been officially rejected by bipartisan groups in the USA.

Again, however, it has proved very hard to convince the wider public otherwise. Indeed, one survey suggested that the number of people in the USA who believed Iraq had had weapons of mass destruction was actually slightly higher after the war than it was before it.[8] (It is possible there was some cognitive dissonance going on here; people didn't want to admit their country had gone to war without a good reason, so became more likely to believe in the justifications – that is pure speculation, however.)

And despite Obama having released his birth certificate in 2011, some 19 per cent of Americans remain convinced he wasn't born in the USA. According to a 2015 CNN/ORC poll, 29 per cent of Americans (including 43 per cent of Republicans) also said they thought he was a Muslim.

Psychologists like Lewandowsky have been turning their experimental skills in recent years to the question of how we can best counter this kind of misinformation. One thing is clear: an official correction (even from the highest officials in a country) isn't enough.

It is possible, of course, that the media simply doesn't give as much coverage to the corrections as it did to the original misinformation (which presumably would be a much more headline-grabbing story), and so the corrected version of the story doesn't reach as wide an audience.

However, there is also evidence that providing people with counter information not only doesn't work, but sometimes backfires; people can be resistant to attempts to change their beliefs. A study in the USA found that presenting people with stories about the potential negative impact of climate change could actually result in Republican supporters becoming even less likely to rate climate change policies as important.[9]

Climate change is a particularly interesting example. It is one of the areas in science where there is near consensus amongst the experts (97 per cent of scientists are in agreement), but there are still highly polarised views among the public in certain countries. Interestingly an Ipsos MORI Global Trends analysis in 2014 found that some of the highest levels of scepticism were in the USA, the UK and Australia. Why climate scepticism is so high in these particular countries isn't clear, but probably relates to the ideas made available in the mainstream media in these countries.

A lot of psychology research has recently been directed towards trying to understand why some people are sceptical of climate change, and how they might be persuaded to change their minds.

One straightforward reason for people's scepticism is that they are presented with a lot of counter claims and evidence by companies and politicians with a vested interest (connections to the oil industry, for example) in spreading doubt about climate change. These parties use a variety of tactics to muddy the waters, such as funding a wide variety of groups, including scientific-sounding organisations, to promote misinformation, claiming that the scientific evidence is contradictory, or giving the impression that scientists are divided on the topic. People then get the impression that climate change is not a clear-cut issue.

Another important factor appears to be what we think others believe. One study in Australia showed that only 283 out of 5,000 people (6 per cent) thought climate change wasn't happening, but those 283 people estimated that around 43 per cent of people shared their climate scepticism – a serious overestimation. On the other hand, nearly 50 per cent of people agreed that man-made climate change was happening, and that group also estimated that only around 40 per cent of the population shared their view.[10]

One of the potential reasons for this discrepancy is that, as we don't generally have direct access to what other people think on a mass scale, we typically rely on the impression we get from various forms of media. This in turn means that the way climate change is reported, often allowing for coverage of both sides of the argument, can skew our view of the topic.

Some media have acknowledged in recent years that their attempts to provide balance on the issue of climate change may have inadvertently contributed to the persistence of climate scepticism. If, in the interests of balance, a media outlet invites a climate sceptic every time they interview a climate scientist, then really the media is giving a false impression that the scientists, and the scientific evidence, are evenly divided. *Last Week Tonight with John Oliver* in the USA illustrated this by showing what a truly balanced debate should look like, inviting three climate sceptics and ninety-seven climate scientists onto the show.

So how can people be persuaded to change their minds?

Cambridge psychologist Sander van der Linden has been looking at what influences our opinions.[11] He and his colleagues have found that people are more likely to accept the evidence of climate science if they first understand the extent of consensus among the scientific community.

However, the effect of highlighting this consensus can be undermined if people are also exposed to misinformation on the topic, such as The Oregon Global Warming Petition Project. This project, often cited by journalists and still making the rounds on social media, claimed 'over 31,000 American scientists have signed a petition stating that there is no scientific evidence that the human release of carbon dioxide will, in the foreseeable future, cause catastrophic heating of the Earth's atmosphere'.

Van der Linden and his colleagues found that they could counteract the misinformation by informing people that 'some politically motivated groups use misleading tactics to try to convince the public that there is a lot of disagreement among scientists'. What was much more effective, however, was providing a detailed critique of the misinformation, for example highlighting that 'some of the signatories are fraudulent, including Charles Darwin and members of the Spice Girls, that fewer than 1% of the signatories have a background in atmospheric/

climate science'. This was effective across the political spectrum in the USA, and had a similar influence on Democrats, Republicans and independents.

The researchers argued that misinformation on climate change is like a virus that can spread through contact – as more people share it and start to believe it. They suggest that people can be 'inoculated' against the virus, by providing detailed information and rebuttals to counter the claims spread by what they call the 'merchants of doubt'.

This is a promising piece of research in some ways as it shows campaigners how to communicate with people in order to change their perceptions. It also, however, highlights the difficulties of doing so if campaigners have to specifically refute all the instances of misinformation that people might have encountered.

$$\boxed{\textit{X}}$$

We need to be able to rely on experts in order to make meaningful decisions, but knowing who to trust and what to believe isn't always clear. The ease with which fake news can spread on social media should be a major concern for us all – no one wants to be taken in by outright lies or find out they've cast their vote based on completely false information.

Unfortunately, the outbreak of fake news has happened at a time when the mainstream media is littered with 'fake experts', and even scientific literature has its share of 'fake science'. In the current climate, we certainly need to approach information we come across with a degree of scepticism – but if that scepticism is applied to topics like vaccines or climate science, as we've seen, it can lead to very negative political and social consequences.

There are some signs of hope; the scientific community is stepping up to the challenge of producing, and disseminating, more reliable evidence, and large organisations like Facebook, Google and Wikipedia are starting to take their responsibilities more seriously.

Ultimately, however, societies that value free speech will never be able to completely prevent fake news from spreading. So we are probably going to have to take some action ourselves and ensure that we check the reliability of our sources, assess the plausibility of shocking stories, and be aware of the ways others might be trying to influence and mislead us.

7

ARE YOU BEING NUDGED?

If you live in Leeds Central, a constituency that has been a Labour stronghold since its creation in 1983, you might have seen an advert on Facebook in the run-up to the 2017 UK general election that was created by the Conservative Party, but didn't mention Conservative policies or politicians. Instead it featured former Labour voters explaining why they were stepping away from their party to vote Tory. One woman said: 'Jeremy Corbyn would be disastrous as a leader and I cannot see him around the negotiating table.'

Meanwhile, immediately to the south in the constituency of Morley and Outwood, voters were treated to a very different advert. In the 2015 election in that constituency, Conservative Andrea Jenkyns had narrowly beaten Labour's former Shadow Chancellor Ed Balls, with UKIP candidate David Dews in third place. This time round voters reported seeing a Conservative video in which Boris Johnson urged UKIP supporters to back the Tories. He said: 'If you vote UKIP, I'm afraid that will be doing exactly what Jeremy Corbyn and Diane Abbott want to happen because it will make it more likely they are in charge.'

Why did these two neighbouring constituencies see such different messages? Because political campaigns are increasingly using social media to reach voters in particular locations, customising messages to appeal directly to those people. And it's not just geography they can target – it's also your age, sex, tastes, preferences and personality.

Across the country, voters reported seeing targeted ads on social media for political parties, including Labour, the Liberal Democrats, the Green Party and the Scottish National Party. Welcome to the brave new world of 'dark ads', where parties can pay Facebook to make sure certain ads are only seen by certain people. A party could design one advert for people under thirty-five, for example, and another for those over thirty-five, and each age group would see only the one that the party has decided best aligns with their political viewpoints.

The idea that parties use tailored messages and other tools to manipulate us is nothing new.

Political insiders have long used so-called 'dog whistle' messages, intended to say different things to different voters. But modern technology is allowing campaigners to take this to a completely different level. The internet, and social media in particular, has opened up what can be a hugely powerful channel not just to communicate with us, but to use our online footprint to analyse and target us – it could be a game-changer for those who can afford to exploit it.

Most of us seem to have accepted the idea that big companies are sharing vast amounts of personal data in order to target us more effectively with advertising. Like me, I'm sure you've browsed items of, say, furniture online only to see adverts for the same items pop up on other sites later. But people are often less aware that political campaigns can also use our online activity to target us with their messages – something that is potentially much more unsettling.

Following the 2016 Brexit referendum and US presidential election, rumours started to swirl about a little-known company named Cambridge Analytica. At the time of writing, this company offers what they call 'data-driven campaigns'. 'By knowing your electorate better,' their marketing materials boast, 'we achieve greater influence while lowering overall costs.' Today, however, the company has become more widely known for supposedly having used psychological profiling based on social media activity to help target campaign material for the 2016 Trump and Brexit campaigns. But what exactly the company did and how successful it was remains the subject of speculation.

CEO Alexander Nix has boasted of the company's 'secret sauce' algorithms, which could predict voters' psychological profiles, but others (including current and former employees) have dismissed such claims as nothing new: crafting different messages to voters depending on their particular profiles is something politicians have been doing for a long time, after all.

As a scientist, but also as a concerned citizen, what is extremely troubling for me is that it is hard to judge the effectiveness of the most recent campaigns as we simply don't know what they are doing. British election campaigns are strictly regulated; unlike America, Canada and Australia, parties and politicians are not allowed to advertise on TV and radio, only on billboards, in newspapers and via election pamphlets. Messages on TV are only allowed through national PPBs – party political broadcasts – TV slots (usually around five minutes long) allocated free of charge using a formula set by Parliament. But those regulations have not yet caught up with – indeed they don't even mention – social media, which is consequently much murkier territory. We also don't know to what extent these companies are trying to oversell their abilities or past successes in order to promote their brand and products.

So what do we know?

Well, whether or not companies like Cambridge Analytica are exaggerating their achievements, their claims are certainly based on some valid scientific foundations.

We know that a data scientist can use your activity on social media sites such as Facebook and Twitter to make accurate guesses about your personality. We also know (as we discussed in Chapter 2) that there are surprising links between our personalities and how we vote.

So yes, in theory, by analysing our activity on social media, campaigns might be able to identify who is most likely to vote for them, and then target campaign material at those people.

We also know from earlier chapters that 'openness to new experiences' is a particularly important dimension to personality when it comes to predicting how we vote. Research by Michal Kosinski and colleagues at the Psychometrics Centre at the University of Cambridge demonstrated that this was something you could accurately guess from people's social media activity.

The researchers created software called ApplyMagicSauce. This software attempts to predict a lot about you, including your age, gender, sexual orientation, personality profile and, importantly, your political leaning. If you look up the website (applymagicsauce. com) and connect it to your Facebook or Twitter account you can see what it says about you.

It may not get everything spot on (it got my age, gender and politics right, but my sexual orientation wrong) but on average, testing hundreds of people, it is impressively accurate. In one of the 100 most influential papers published in 2015, the software proved more accurate in describing someone's personality profile than a close friend.[1]

The software requires sophisticated algorithms that detect patterns in data using millions of observations that would be too subtle for humans ever to detect themselves. It can only make an accurate guess about you based on your online activity, however, so the more you do online, the more accurate its prediction of your personality. If you've only ever liked a few things on Facebook, for example, the algorithms won't have a lot to go on and are about as accurate in guessing your personality as a work colleague would be. After around 70 'likes', however, they perform (on average) better than a friend would. After 100 likes, the software can outperform a family member.

And, rather incredibly, after 300 likes it can describe your personality profile more accurately than your partner can!

Running and interpreting these algorithms means paying for experts in data processing and analysis. This in turn means that political campaigns with more cash to spend on data science might have an advantage in identifying and reaching receptive voters. There is also some speculation that campaigns are using the same techniques to identify voters who are likely to support the other side, then targeting them with campaign material intended to deter them from voting, such as by attempting to discredit particular politicians, or creating cynicism in the political process.

Overall Donald Trump spent far less on his campaign than Hillary Clinton did on hers, but he spent a lot more than she did on social media. By the end of the campaign, Trump's digital team was estimated to have spent around $85 million on digital and online advertising. It is also estimated that Trump's campaign made hundreds of thousands of different pieces of creative content, testing and refining their messages.

Wired journalist Issie Lapowsky spoke to Gary Coby, a member of Trump's digital team and director of advertising at the Republican National Committee: 'On any given day, Coby says, the campaign was running 40,000 to 50,000 variants of its ads ... On the day of the third presidential debate in October, the team ran 175,000 variations.'

We don't know exactly what they were doing with all of those ad variants, but it is possible that they were targeting voters based on their psychological profile. And there are some areas where using psychological profiling clearly might have helped. For example, people who score lower on openness to new experiences are more likely to be receptive to messages about controlling immigration – so the best way to engage them might therefore be to target them on that particular subject.

Writing about Cambridge Analytica and the Trump campaign, *New York Times* reporters Nicholas Confessore and Danny Hakim explained how they thought voters might be targeted: 'A voter deemed neurotic might be shown a gun-rights commercial featuring burglars breaking into a home, rather than a defense of the Second Amendment; political ads warning of the dangers posed by the Islamic State could be targeted directly at voters prone to anxiety.'

Trump also made a clear appeal to a sense of national pride, with his call to 'make America great again'. Had I been working for a data firm for Trump's campaign, I would have been trying to target voters with the strongest sense of in-group loyalty, who would be the most receptive to that message.

Another core group that Trump appealed to was white working-class voters who saw global trade agreements and outsourcing as a threat to their jobs. If Trump's campaign had also used demographic data (such as age, gender, occupation) to identify and target such voters with his messages about bringing jobs back to America and protecting US industries, you can start to see how an effective modern digital campaign might work.

Again, however, the big problem is that while there is clear evidence behind the idea of psychological profiling, there is still a big gap between that knowledge and what campaigns are doing in real life.

During the 2017 UK election, a group of 'political technologists' in London set out to develop software that would reveal what political campaigns are doing on social media. They created a plug-in called Who Targets Me – citizens in the UK could install this plug-in, and it would automatically send the developers information about any targeted political adverts directed to those voters. This platform is therefore designed to help bring 'dark ads' into the light, so that we can compare what messages are being targeted to different users in different parts of the country.

The developers are themselves calling for clearer regulation of online political campaigning, but in the meantime this 'hack' will hopefully offer a little bit of insight into what political parties are doing online. At the time of writing these results are still being analysed, but one thing that seems clear already is that some parties, particularly the Liberal Democrats, are doing a lot of A/B testing with their messages. This is a classic technique in behavioural research on marketing; two (or more) similar messages are developed, both are then released and assessed on a limited basis, and then the more effective of the two versions is rolled out.

But what also seems to be clear is that these British efforts are amateurish by comparison with what the Americans were doing the year before: Gary Coby referred to his team's approach for the Trump campaign as 'A/B testing on steroids'.

On one level this seems like a fairly harmless way of increasing the efficiency of political campaigns, helping parties develop effective messaging as quickly as possible. Indeed, you could argue that this strategy could help campaigns engage more voters on the issues that matter most to them. Given all that we have learned about confirmation biases, however, it also means campaigns could end up feeding us the messages we want to hear, rather than enabling us to make a genuinely informed vote.

There are also some reports suggesting that the UK Labour Party (after rather neglecting the use of social media in 2015), has started integrating its 'on the ground' and 'online' campaigns. Apparently, if you mention concerns about the NHS to a Labour canvasser on the doorstep, you might find adverts about Labour's stance on the NHS appearing in your Facebook newsfeed later that day.

But does that really matter? After all, we've seen that it's not that easy to change someone's mind. Indeed, the conventional wisdom in modern election campaigns is that you shouldn't focus on trying to convince people on the other side. You should instead aim for the political centre where the so-called 'swing voters' are likely to be found – and most importantly ensure that your base actually turns out to vote. Most of the 'door-knocking' by party canvassers in the run-up to an election is about identifying people who already support their party to ensure they come out to vote on election day.

As it turns out, however, with a little bit of psychological insight, campaigns might be able to achieve a lot more than that. In the previous chapter, I mentioned a study that suggested it was possible to change people's views on a polarising topic (the kind of topic that can shape how people vote) just by having a canvasser talk to them for a few minutes. Two scientists exposed this study for being based on false data, but when they finished running their own study, on transgender discrimination, their results showed that the canvassing strategy really can change people's biases on a particular topic.[2] The data used in the first study may have been false buts its findings were not.

There was no dispute about the second study's validity: the researchers found that sending canvassers to talk to people for ten minutes about how transgender people suffered from prejudice substantially reduced transphobia, and the effects were still evident three months later.

The two researchers cautioned against the received wisdom of only focusing on voters who already agree with you, concluding instead that it may be in campaigns' best interests to engage people across partisan lines, even on controversial topics. In this instance the researchers encouraged voters to 'take the perspective' of transgender individuals, but it is plausible that on other key topics there are also messages or techniques that might be particularly effective in changing people's minds. Indeed, in the previous chapter we saw how the message that '97% of climate scientists agree that man-made climate change is happening' has been identified as a key 'gateway' belief in changing people's minds on this hot topic.

Perhaps political parties have in fact been aiming too low. Perhaps they should be designing campaigns to try to change beliefs and attitudes on key issues rather than simply getting their base to turn out. What is certainly clear is that as the science of why we vote the way we do advances, political parties are likely to turn to increasingly more sophisticated ways of winning our vote.

$$\boxed{x}$$

The use of psychological insights to target voters on social media is a relatively recent step, but attempts to use psychology to influence citizens' behaviour in other ways stretch back over at least the last fifteen years – and have developed rapidly in that time. Government departments and policy-makers are increasingly aware that a little bit of psychological insight can go a long way in changing what people do. So much so that the approach has a name: nudge (from the book of the same name by Cass R. Sunstein and Richard H. Thaler).

So, what does 'nudge' mean in this context?

The underlying logic of the nudge agenda (also referred to as 'behavioural insights') is that by understanding why people behave the way they do, we may be able to subtly 'nudge' them, using very small adjustments, to make particular choices. Famously, the urinals at Schiphol Airport in Amsterdam painted a fly next to the drain holes and reduced spillage by 80 per cent. 'It turns out that, if you give men a target, they can't help but aim at it,' wrote Sunstein and Thaler.

The idea is not to try to force people into doing things they might not otherwise have done, but rather to encourage choices that people themselves would agree are beneficial. A lot of nudge projects look at the ways in which governments communicate with people, to make those systems as efficient as possible. For example, in the UK the NHS has tested various ways of sending people different kinds of letters, emails and even timely and personalised texts to make sure they turn up to their hospital appointments on time. And governments in the USA and UK have both used the 'nudge' approach to get people to save for their pensions and pay their taxes on time.

Not surprisingly, it isn't just governments that are making use of such psychological insights. Technology companies are also trying to understand how to change our behaviour. Most of the time these changes are simply aimed at improving the company's profits. Some companies, however, are also exploring how they could help promote civic engagement.

In 2012, researchers from Facebook published a paper in collaboration with a team from the University of California that demonstrated the power the social network has both to experiment on its users and to influence elections.[3] On the day of the 2010 US congressional elections, Facebook presented millions of users with a clickable 'I voted' button at the top of their newsfeed (you may well have seen a similar button if you used Facebook on the day of the 2017 general election in the UK).

However, in that election not everybody saw the same thing. One group of people were just given the option of clicking on the button to show friends that they had voted, while other users also saw the profile pictures of some friends who had already clicked the 'I voted' button themselves.

The study demonstrated that voters who saw the 'I voted' button along with an image of any friends who had pressed this button, were more likely to click on it themselves than those who simply saw the button. And the closer the friends, the more likely people were to follow suit. Even more importantly, using public voter records (in the USA there is a public record of who voted, although not who they voted for) the researchers argued that the people who saw that their close friends had pressed the button were also more likely to actually vote.

The researchers estimated that by placing this simple button on people's news feeds, Facebook may have increased turnout rates by something in the order of 60,000 votes. In a closer contest, such as the famously tight race between George W. Bush and Al Gore back in 2000, this small social nudge could have been enough to change the result of an election. And given that Facebook use is still higher among younger generations, who are more likely to vote to the left, this 'politically neutral' attempt by a social media channel to increase voter participation could have inadvertently nudged the vote in favour of the Democrats.

This result demonstrates an important principle in the science of behaviour change. Namely, if you want something to be effective in changing people's behaviour, make it social. It might seem crude or gimmicky to promote voting using online 'peer pressure' but such action actually has roots in the past: in Italy there used to be a tradition of pinning the names of all voters to the front door of the town hall (to show who had lived up to their civic duty). As we will see, there is much more that exponents of psychology could do to develop civic rituals like this to promote voting.

Many people criticised Facebook for the experiment described above and for other such large-scale trials (which were all carried out without informing users – who automatically give their consent to be experimented on when they agree to the terms and conditions of service), arguing that they are manipulating users and potentially influencing election outcomes.

The reality is that large tech companies such as Facebook, Amazon and Google are constantly trying things out on us on us, working out what combinations of adverts or posts are more likely to keep us using their sites, and engaging with things that make them money – and of course how best to use the huge amounts of data that they have about each of us. It's just that we normally don't see the results. In this instance, the fact that Facebook published the results of their experiment so openly could be said to count in their favour, and it could also be argued that they were attempting to encourage something that almost everyone would agree is a positive outcome: higher voter turnout.

In fact there is so much consensus on the importance of increasing turnout that there has been a lot of non-partisan academic research aimed at trying to understand what does and doesn't work.

One of the most famous studies in this area highlighted something very similar to Facebook's experiment, namely that social pressure matters. In 2006, leading political scientists Alan Gerber and colleagues at Yale University set out to test whether they could increase voter participation in a Michigan state election by writing to potential voters with different messages, applying varying degrees of pressure to vote.[4] Some citizens received a standard letter encouraging them to do their civic duty; others were informed that their voting records were being studied; and one group received a letter explaining that after the election, another letter would be sent with a complete list of everybody who had and hadn't voted on that street so that 'you and your neighbors will all know who voted and who did not'.

The results were both dramatic and depressing. The usual level of voting was 29.7 per cent, but for those in the 'neighbours' group this shot up to 37.8 per cent – a proportional increase of almost 30 per cent. Quite a dramatic effect for a simple letter – and a vastly larger one than was achieved in the Facebook study. The cost of sending everyone a letter was certainly higher than putting a button on voters' Facebook feeds, but it was much cheaper and less labour-intensive than traditional door-knocking or phone-bank approaches.

At the same time the study also highlights just how low levels of voter participation can be, and how sad it is that we might regard 37.8 per cent as a successful outcome. Perhaps it only seems successful compared to other attempts to get people to vote: the letter reminding people of their civic duty to vote only increased voting levels to 31.5 per cent. But this does demonstrate the importance of testing the effectiveness of different ways of campaigning. All too often well-meaning campaigners will try to promote some agenda (like voting, recycling, taking public transport), but make no attempt to test whether their campaign will actually make any difference.

So, knowing your neighbours will find out whether you have voted seems to be a much greater motivation than being reminded of your civic duty. Humans are very susceptible to what other humans are doing, and to what other humans will think they are doing.

However, although it is interesting that social pressure can influence our behaviour, the psychological elephant in the room is really why so many people don't vote at all. Other experiments have demonstrated ways to encourage us into the ballot booth, from voter registration lotteries[5] to canvassing campaigns, phone banks and leaflets,[6] but most of the effects are rather small. From a psychological perspective the more important question is why any of this is even necessary in the first place. If humans are such inherently social animals, why do so many of us not participate in what is probably one of the most influential collective acts of communication we get to make?

8

A SILENT MAJORITY

Most people seemed to agree that 2016 turned out to be a political rollercoaster of a year. After the shock result of the EU referendum and Donald Trump's rise to the US presidency, there was a sense of fatigue in the air; many of us seemed to be worn out by it all.

So when UK Prime Minister Theresa May performed a startling U-turn on her previously stated position and suddenly called a general election for June 2017 – a mere two years after the 2015 election and less than twelve months since the EU referendum – the nation's reaction seemed to be summed up by 'Brenda from Bristol' who gave this now famous response to a BBC news reporter: 'You're joking? Not another one? Oh for God's sake,

I can't stand this. There's too much politics going on at the moment. Why does she need to do it?'

With that feeling in the air, there were fears that voter turnout would be low.

Over the last fifty years, the general trend in many Western democracies has been for levels of voting to decline (except in countries like Belgium or Australia where it is compulsory, and failing to do so can result in a fine). Despite the fact that many people consider voting to be an almost sacrosanct civic responsibility, in democracies all over the world it is a right that millions of people regularly choose not to exercise.

Yet the number of people who voted in the British 2017 general election was – to the pollsters' surprise – the highest in twenty-five years at 68.7 per cent (an increase of 2.6 per cent on the 2015 election, although still a long way off the 1950 figure of 83.9 per cent).

That seems like good news, but it masks a depressing truth.

For while the Conservatives may have won the largest share of the votes, with 42 per cent, that still means that only 29.2 per cent of the registered electorate voted for them, while 27.5 per cent opted for Labour. After accounting for all the smaller parties, that leaves the actual majority share with the non-voters, at 31.3 per cent – well over 14 million people.

In short, more people chose not to exercise their democratic right than voted for the party that won the election.

This non-voting majority sits in quite a stark contrast to the efforts of different disenfranchised parts of society – the working classes in the UK, black citizens in the USA and women all over the world, to name a few – who fought, and in some cases died, for the right to vote.

We've seen a number of ways in which the way we vote might be influenced. But what might make us choose not to vote at all, to disregard a privilege to which so many people across the globe still don't have access?

$$\boxed{\text{✗}}$$

One of the most common explanations for low voter turnout is that people are lazy or apathetic. As a psychologist, I struggle with this explanation. When people say they don't care about politics, often what they mean is that they don't care about the day-to-day workings of the government or politicians' activities, but when it comes to how much nurses are paid, or who receives benefits, or whether very rich people are paying their share of taxes, most people do care.

Over the years I've talked to a lot of non-voters, and the reasons I hear most often are that they don't feel they know enough to vote meaningfully, they don't feel any of the parties really represent them, they don't trust politicians, or they don't even want to legitimise the political process.

But these are just anecdotal observations; what evidence is there to back any of them up? Let's start with the problem of people feeling they don't know enough about the political system.

One clear finding is that a lack of political engagement often goes hand-in-hand with dramatic gaps in people's understanding of the political process. The Hansard Society has conducted an 'Engagement Audit' every year since 2004, documenting the levels of engagement and political knowledge in the UK. Some of the results are rather shocking; a regular finding, for example, is that less than half of the people they survey can name their local Member of Parliament. In 2013, just 22 per cent were able to do so.

Likewise, in 2007, 2010 and 2013 the survey results suggested that as little as half the population understood that as citizens of the EU they could directly elect their Members of the European Parliament. Yet in 2016 these same citizens were tasked with taking the momentous decision about whether or not Britain should leave the EU.

Such low levels of political knowledge are concerning, and the question of how to raise them an important one. Perhaps the problem partly stems from the fact we're generally not taught about politics from a young age. In 2002, this gap in the curriculum was at least partially addressed by the introduction of 'citizenship' as a compulsory part of state-run secondary school education, but this does not apply to independent schools, academies or free schools, so its impact has been reduced accordingly. It is certainly true that for members of older generations such as myself, there was a really quite shocking absence of politics education at school.

Admittedly, teaching civics and politics in school is fraught with complications, particularly the issue of how to make sure the topic is taught without bias. At the same time, however, I wasn't taught even the most basic aspects of how my democracy works, such as the distinction between the roles of a councillor, a Member of Parliament and a Member of the European Parliament. We are simply expected to pick this kind of information up for ourselves – and many people do – but surely far more people would feel engaged with our often complex political systems if we were taught the fundamentals at school.

Perhaps unsurprisingly then, there is a link between educational level and levels of voter participation. Those who achieve a higher level of education are more likely to vote. They also tend to know more about the political process, and perhaps therefore how to navigate it. It is fair to say, however, that the effects of this link are more pronounced in some countries than others, which suggests that there are other factors also at play. For example, in both Sweden and the USA, having a university degree is associated with a better grasp of politics, but there's a much bigger difference in political knowledge between educated and uneducated people in the USA than there is in Sweden. Perhaps this has something to do with the fact that Sweden is in general a much more egalitarian society, which could mean that differences in education result have a less pronounced effect.[1]

There is also some evidence that the type of media we choose to consume reflects our level of political knowledge. US citizens who preferred the 'news' over 'entertainment' were more likely to know about politics and more likely to vote.[2] That hardly seems surprising, but the relation between engagement in politics and knowledge of politics is actually something of a chicken and egg issue. It's difficult to know whether people don't engage in politics because they have such a low understanding of it to begin with, or whether they have such a low understanding because they have no interest in engaging with it. The reality is almost certainly a messy interaction between these factors. But whatever the mechanics of the interaction, it does seem that the first step in convincing people to cast a vote is making sure they understand the system they are supposed to be participating in.

⊠

Of course, the fact that people choose not to vote can't simply be explained by how well they know the system. Some people are happy to cast a vote despite not knowing how it all works, and some people abstain even though they do.

Another way people have tried to explain it is by looking at individual characteristics to see whether there are any traits associated with non-voters. One of the most interesting studies in this area comes from an organisation called the Common Cause Foundation. It was set up by Tom Crompton who, having worked on environmental campaigns for the World Wildlife Foundation for many years, wanted to understand the values that make people care about the world around them. After the 2015 election in the UK, Crompton ran a large survey of the UK population to try to understand, in particular, the values associated with the decision to vote.[3]

The study asked people whether they felt 'compassionate' values (honesty, responsibility, equality) or 'selfish' values (wealth, social status, popularity) were more important to them, and which ones they thought were important to others. The results showed that those with more 'selfish' values were slightly less likely to vote.

But Crompton also found that only a minority of people rated 'selfish' values as more important than 'compassionate' ones (and that was true for liberals and conservatives), with 74 per cent holding compassionate values overall. Interestingly, though, the result did vary across different age groups; older age groups were much more likely to endorse more compassionate values. This clearly corresponds with the fact that older generations are more likely to vote, a fact we will return to later in the chapter.

So much for the values that people considered important to themselves. What about when they were asked about what 'others' valued?

Well, it turned out that most people overestimated the extent to which others prioritised selfish values – it seems we assume others are more selfish than they really are. Interestingly, this finding also correlated with whether or not people voted: those who thought other people tended to have selfish values were also less likely to vote.

What do these findings tell us?

It seems fairly straightforward to explain why people who endorse more selfish values would be less likely to vote: voting takes effort, and perhaps those people are prone to being a little bit lazy and simply can't be bothered to head out to the polling booth. Then again, political parties often appeal to the self-interests of different voters, so if one party offers you a tax-break, or free education, or a higher state pension, then you could imagine a selfish person being even more likely to vote. So it's not that simple.

The second result is even more intriguing. Why would thinking that others are selfish make you less likely to vote?

It's certainly a curious finding, but it is consistent with something we have seen throughout this book: what (we think) other people think matters to us – if we think our neighbours will know whether or not we voted, for example, or if we believe a large proportion of people buy into climate scepticism – this can have an effect on our behaviour. Why should the perception of others' selfish values make a difference to whether or not we vote? In all honesty, I don't know – this is definitely one of those cases where, as we scientists often say, 'more research is needed ...' – but I would like to offer one potential explanation.

If you are intending to vote, and especially if you are going to vote in line with compassionate values, then you probably need a certain degree of faith that others share those values. Otherwise you may worry whether your vote will make a difference. To put it another way, if you want to vote for a more compassionate society, but think you are surrounded by people who will vote out of self-interest, then you might decide your vote is likely to be wasted. Perhaps, for some people at least, the decision to vote requires some degree of faith that collective action can bring about change.

Again, I want to make clear, this explanation is speculative, but it does rely on two factors that we know to be important: the role of faith and cynicism in the political process, and a sense of 'perceived control'.

$$\boxed{\textbf{\textit{X}}}$$

The idea that 'my vote won't make a difference' is one that is frequently expressed in politics. Indeed, some statisticians in the USA have calculated that if you go to the voting booths, the chances of you getting run over are slightly higher than the chances of you influencing the outcome of an election.

Perhaps that's true on an individual level, but collectively, if every non-voter became a voter, they could obviously make a huge difference – although we can't of course predict in what direction. (It is certainly true that low voter turnout can lead to surprising results. For example in the UK, the United Kingdom Independence Party (UKIP) is a relatively minor party, with no MPs, but with turnout in European elections being so low (35.6 per cent), it actually won the most seats in the 2014 elections for UK Members of the European Parliament.)

The depressingly low levels of political engagement in the UK are associated with a degree of cynicism about politicians and the political process, as the surveys conducted by the Hansard Society have repeatedly found.

This brings us to the idea that psychologists call 'perceived control' (political scientists tend to refer to it as 'perceived efficacy'). How much control people feel they have over their lives is important in many situations – from the work place[4] to schools.[5] A recent paper in *Cognition* has found evidence that just realising you have control over something can be inherently rewarding in its own right.[6] The authors argue this sense of reward could help to explain why millions of people use their limited time and money playing computer games like 'Candy Crush Saga'. Simple games like this give us a sense of control – we're able to very quickly work out what we need to do to gain points and rewards, and progress in the game, granting a kind of instant gratification for our desire to feel in control.

So how does perceived control affect our voting habits?

Well, we know that there is a clear link between how much people feel their individual vote counts and how likely they are to vote. We know this because we can compare the different voting systems countries use, which affect how likely an individual's vote is to have a direct impact on who gets elected.

The USA and the UK, for example, both rely on a 'winner takes all' system, whereby in each local area the person with the most votes wins. This system (commonly referred to as 'first past the post') means that a political party could gain 10 per cent of the vote in every constituency in the country, and end up with no representatives in parliament, so long as another party got at least 11 per cent or more in each seat.

That means that in many parts of the country, particularly if you live in a so-called 'safe seat' (an area where one party has a consistently large majority that is unlikely to change), your vote is unlikely to make a difference. Perhaps unsurprisingly, turnout is much lower in safe seats.[7]

Conversely, if you live in a seat where the margin between the parties is very narrow, then your sense of control over the process is going to be higher, making you much more likely to vote. As an interesting aside, in these 'marginal' seats, voters also tend to have higher levels of political knowledge, perhaps suggesting that in safe-seat areas people feel it's not worth getting involved, as the result is a foregone conclusion. Politicians know it too; voters in marginal constituencies are far more likely to be targeted by political parties, increasing the feeling that their vote counts, as opposed to voters in safe seats who frequently complain of being ignored and overlooked.

Many other democracies use a 'proportional' system; there are numerous versions but the basic idea is that if 10 per cent of the people vote for one party, then that party will end up with 10 per cent of the representatives in parliament.

Across the world, democracies with more proportional systems have higher levels of voter turnout, such as Germany (71 per cent), the Netherlands (80 per cent) and Denmark (88 per cent). Interestingly, voters in those countries are more likely to say they feel they have a sense of control over the electoral process.[8] This is particularly true for voters who want to support smaller parties, and it's a fairly logical consequence of proportional systems, as smaller parties (like the Green Party in Germany) are able to get more representatives in parliament. In contrast, the Green Party in the UK got 3.8 per cent of the vote in the 2015 'first past the post' election but only gained 0.15 per cent of the seats in parliament, and UKIP got 12.7 per cent of the vote but only 0.3 per cent of the seats, while the SNP got 50 per cent of the vote in Scotland and a huge 95 per cent of the seats.

There are two interesting points to note here. Firstly, the higher levels of support for smaller parties in countries that use proportional representation demonstrates quite clearly that political beliefs do not simply cluster into a simple left- and right-wing party system – as they have traditionally done in the USA and UK. In Germany, for instance, there are a range of different parties, and support for them seems to be based on a more complex and subtle association between their stance on certain policies and the different personality traits of voters. For example, if a person scores highly on Openness, they are slightly more likely to support parties that endorse social liberalism; whereas a person with high levels of Neuroticism (those low on emotional stability) is slightly more likely to support parties that promote policies protecting against cultural challenges.[9]

Second, a person's decision to vote is both a reflection of their individual characteristics and the nature of the voting system in which they find themselves. People will respond differently depending on the level of control they feel they have in different contexts.

There have been two recent examples of votes in the UK that offered people a greater sense of control: the 2014 Scottish independence referendum, and the 2016

EU referendum. The most obvious thing to note about both is that turnout was much higher than for normal parliamentary elections. No less than 84.6 per cent of voters turned out for the Scottish referendum, for example, and 72.2 per cent voted across England, Wales, Scotland and Northern Ireland for the Brexit vote, compared to an average of 66.1 per cent turnout for the 2015 general election.

It seems that when people get the chance to vote directly on an issue of clear importance, they are more likely to make the effort to vote. It also appears that this boost in engagement can sometimes have knock-on effects; for example in the 2015 UK election, the turnout in Scotland was 71.1 per cent, much higher than in England, Wales and Northern Ireland. This post-referendum effect might also help to explain why (despite Brenda of Bristol's voter fatigue) turnout in the UK's 2017 election was relatively high.

$$\boxed{\textbf{\textit{X}}}$$

Another reason for the increased turnout in the 2017 UK election was because the younger generations (18 to 24 year olds) got more involved. Traditionally they're accused of being too lazy and/or disengaged, and politicians tend to have stopped targeting them. And it is true that in 2015 the turnout among this age group was just 44 per cent.

But clearly we can't simply dismiss them as 'lazy'; after all it is unlikely that between 2015 and 2017 the youth of the UK underwent a radical shift in personality. No, what changed was the political context. Younger voters had already engaged in greater numbers than predicted in the 2016 referendum, a vote that saw stark differences across different generations (with over 70 per cent of 18 to 24 year olds voting to remain, while 64 per cent of those aged 65 and over voted to leave). The Labour Party then very explicitly targeted younger voters, with registration drives, using social media to bypass the mainstream media, and policies aimed at younger generations (such as educational allowances and free university tuition).

Most political pundits assumed this strategy wouldn't work; the established wisdom was that the young don't turn out, no matter what efforts campaigners go to. But the youth proved the pundits wrong (yet another incorrect prediction by our 'experts'!). It seems that over the generations a negative cycle had built up whereby small differences in turnout between age groups were exacerbated by parties progressively focusing less and less on younger voters, leaving them less and less likely to vote.

☒

The ways in which we can engage with and learn about democracy are changing. We have already seen that political parties are increasingly turning to social media as a means of winning our vote. We've also seen how the type of media a person consumes is linked to how likely they are to vote. However, this particular finding was published just before the explosion of media diversity via outlets such as Facebook and Twitter.

We don't know what effect social media might have, but it's possible that the ability to share information and collectively organise online might facilitate 'non-traditional' forms of participation in politics, such as the signing of e-petitions. This is one means of engaging in the political system that has been on the rise in countries around the world, even though voter turnout has been declining over the last fifty years.

Signing e-petitions, or 'clicktivism' as it has been derogatorily dubbed, has been dismissed by some as a lazy substitute for real participation. But I think that is a little premature. Whether modern 'clicktivism' has the potential to effect real, long-term change is yet to be seen, but it is certainly attracting certain demographics that have traditionally been less likely to engage in the political process; younger age groups and women are far more likely to sign and distribute e-petitions for example, as well as taking part in a range of other 'non-traditional' forms of engagement like protests and consumer boycotts.[10]

Former UK Prime Minster David Cameron responded to this trend in 2011 by launching an official petitions page on the parliamentary website. A senior figure in the House of Commons said this platform would offer the general public a 'megaphone' to make their views heard in parliament. Cameron guaranteed as much by decreeing that petitions with over 100,000 signatures would be debated in the House of Commons. In the first year alone, the petitions added to the site attracted 6.4 million signatures.

Although the public has clearly engaged with these e-petitions, we don't know what the long-term impacts of this will be. If people feel that large-scale petitions are taken seriously and responded to meaningfully, then this could act as a 'foot in the door' for more of us to become politically engaged. At the moment however, even if a petition passes the threshold of 100,000 signatures, it often receives a very perfunctory response, and isn't necessarily debated in the main chamber but in a small committee room with only a handful of MPs present.

If politicians are going to offer platforms like this, then they need to think carefully about how to respond without disillusioning people who are starting to show an interest in how their country is run.

$$\boxed{X}$$

Understanding why some people don't vote at all can sometimes be even harder than trying to understand why they would vote for a party you dislike – especially if you see voting as an important civic duty.

But, just as we have seen in the science of why people *do* vote, there's a lot psychology can tell us about why some of us choose not to.

The voting systems of countries like the USA and UK have resulted in the formation of a silent majority, where many don't feel they have a sense of control over the process. As the political landscape changes, and new forms of engagement emerge, it's interesting to question what might happen if that silent majority were to find its voice.

CONCLUSION: DEMOCRACY FOR HUMANS

There's a chance you've found some of the studies in this book quite surprising. I certainly have. In looking at the wide range of research that is revealing more and more about the 'political animal', I've gained a new sense of perspective on why I vote the way I do. That's how I felt, for example, when I first learnt about the relationship between Openness and political views; it seemed consistent with my own choices, and went some way towards explaining why I favour certain policies that others find so problematic.

Over the last century psychologists have found that we aren't always aware of the reasons why we act the way we do, or make one decision rather than another, especially when those reasons involve complex and subtle factors like differences in our personalities and moral values.

Once you become aware of some of the factors at play, you might also find they help make sense of your experiences and beliefs – both in relation to yourself and to people you know. Of course, most of the findings are only true on average, and there are many reasons why we make certain decisions. But perhaps some of the studies in this book have inspired you to question what your beliefs and ideas are based on – and even whether you want to reassess any of your political choices.

That is all entirely up to you to decide.

The research certainly doesn't tell us whether a particular viewpoint is right or wrong – it can only offer a deeper understanding of ourselves and others.

Take nationalism, for example. Many people believe, quite rationally, that the nation state is a critical part of how the modern world works, and we should each support our nation in the interests of political stability and social cohesion. Others consider in-group loyalty to be an important aspect of morality, shaping their political opinions on issues such as the primacy of their own country and their own people.

There is not one reason why a person believes strongly in the nation state. Perhaps, as a nationalist, you think that your views have nothing to do with in-group loyalty, and that the research on moral psychology could detract from more important reasons for supporting nationalism. However, you might find the research on in-group loyalty gives you some ideas for how to communicate with those who don't share your outlook.

Likewise, if you disagree with the concept of nationalism, this research might give you a better understanding of those who do, and inspire you to find a way of engaging with them. Or it might give you greater confidence to challenge them, and to argue that we shouldn't be guided by a moral intuition that may have evolved in the past and which you don't think is useful today.

Again, that's up to you.

I suspect, however, that many of us would rather not be prone to some of the unconscious biases described in this book. Do we really want a politician's looks to influence our vote? Or to find out that our support for a particular policy depends only on which political party proposes it? Do we want to pay attention only to information that agrees with our outlook, dismissing any evidence to the contrary, no matter how valid? If these were choices we made consciously, then there might be ways we could justify them; but it's the idea that our decisions are being influenced without us even being aware of it that probably makes us feel uncomfortable.

Nevertheless, sometimes these biases do affect our choices. In fact, they are arguably so powerful that you might question how (or whether) democracy can ever really function at all. If you started this book worried about the current political climate, you might now be even more concerned by the way humans can make such a mess of the process. Or maybe you'll now have a little more hope that you can understand those you disagree with.

Whatever your view, we are probably stuck with democracy for the foreseeable future. As Churchill said: 'Democracy is the worst form of government, except for all the others.' So perhaps we need to think about how the system can function best, given the many biases to which we humans seem to be susceptible.

Political scientists have become increasingly concerned about this. One aspect they have considered important when assessing the health of our democracies is the amount of 'correct voting'[1] that takes place – a 'correct' vote being one that matches the values and beliefs of the voter in question. They conclude that actually, most people do vote 'correctly' (although there are various differences across countries and personality types).

Personally, I find the concept of 'correct voting' very problematic; I'm not convinced that academics have a strong enough grasp of the complex interplay of character traits and beliefs that we have explored in this book to be able to judge whether someone has voted 'correctly'. I think the whole approach neglects some of the complications involved in how people's views and beliefs are formed in the first place, and doesn't adequately account for the way people can hold an array of different – and sometimes contradictory – views. It also overlooks the role of the media, especially the way in which it can shape our priorities. And it doesn't address the role of confirmation biases, which can make us cling to our beliefs, even in the face of solid evidence against them.

Then there's the bias that academics themselves bring to the question of 'correct voting'. For a start, many fields in academia are dominated by people with left-wing views. In the 1950s, particularly in psychology, there was a reasonable balance, but nowadays, for every conservative psychology professor in the USA, there are fifteen liberal ones. In fact there is currently some debate over whether or not this poses a fundamental problem for psychology as a field.[2]

Our perspective and biases will inevitably influence everything we do. And that includes the way I have written this book. In this respect, I follow the advice of Ric Bailey, the BBC's chief political adviser, who encourages his journalists to try to become aware of their own biases.

In that spirit, one of the areas in which my own personal interests might bias my thinking revolves around the question of 'perceived control'. I've probably emphasised it more than other researchers might, but (in my opinion) there is a lot of good evidence for its importance. We looked at a few examples in Chapter 8, but here's another one. In a huge study (involving over 3,000 participants) Margie Lachman and Suzanne Weaver looked at how people of different social classes varied in terms of their perceived control, wellbeing and health.[3] Unsurprisingly they found that participants with higher incomes scored highly on all three measures; however, they then showed that low-income participants could have just as high levels of health and wellbeing if they also had a high sense of perceived control.

In other words, if you were a countess ruling the roost in Downton Abbey, you would be likely to enjoy a good measure of control, and high levels of health and well-being. But you might feel no more satisfied than the head butler, as long as he felt, as butlers tend to do, that he had the run of things.

I think this idea of control is often neglected when discussing politics and democracy in society. Democracy isn't just about 'crowd sourcing' opinions on how we should be governed; critically, it offers everybody in society the chance to have some sense of control over the process. And, as we have seen, it is when people feel their vote doesn't make a difference that they can start to feel cynical or disengaged.

It is troubling to think that a third of the electorate in the UK don't vote, and that many of those who do will make their decision based on startlingly little knowledge of the political system. If we want to reverse this trend, education is the most obvious place to start. In the USA, the Civics Education Initiative has been campaigning to make it a requirement in every state for students to pass a civics exam before they can graduate from high school. Of course, teaching politics without bias is a genuine challenge, but there are clearly basic facts about the mechanics of how our democracy works that can be taught – and some of those at least have formed part of the citizenship classes that were introduced to Britain's state secondary schools in 2002. In many places, however, students still finish school knowing very little about how their democracy works, while at the same time being exposed to all sorts of fake news across the internet.

Knowing what or who to trust is probably one of the biggest challenges facing future generations. I think therefore that it isn't enough to teach people how to exercise their democratic right; we must also teach them about the biases that might affect their decisions. (Of course, all academics think that their discipline is the most important and should be prioritised in education – the difference is, psychology really is the most important!) All of us should be aware, for example, that we have a tendency to focus on evidence that supports our views, or that we can start to believe something just because we've have heard it multiple times.

In his 2011 book *The Better Angels of Our Nature*, Harvard psychologist Stephen Pinker argues that over the course of human history, conditions have been steadily improving, with, for example, decreasing levels of violence, poverty and child mortality.[4] But most of us don't seem to have that impression – generally because of what we hear in the media. As we saw in Chapter 5, newspapers and broadcasts tend to focus on negative stories and events ('If it bleeds, it leads', as the old adage goes).

Pinker also argues that there have been particular times in human history where things have improved more rapidly than others, and that one of these was thanks, in part, to the development of the printing press, which made literature much more accessible. As literacy levels rose over the course of the next few centuries, people didn't just have access to more knowledge, but also to other perspectives – with significant results. For example, in eighteenth- and nineteenth-century America, a number of autobiographies and novels were written from the point of view of black slaves, which many argue were highly influential in challenging the prejudice of white Americans, and helped build some of the popular momentum behind the eventual abolition of slavery.

Nowadays, it is even easier to access what other people say, and to see how other people live – but we still find it a challenge to really appreciate other people's outlooks.

I think moral psychology and personality psychology offer a genuine opportunity to better understand the perspective of those we disagree with politically. As I've said already, I don't think this means we will suddenly all start agreeing with each other, but it could help us grasp a little more clearly the points on which we disagree and, perhaps, help us focus instead on areas where we can find some common ground.

I know a lot of people say they dislike talking politics, because the exchanges often become very heated or opinionated. Perhaps the little bit of political psychology in this book will help to make your conversations more constructive – or even more enjoyable. And perhaps we might all find the time to pause every once in a while and ask ourselves: what's my bias?

NOTES

Chapter 1: It's Not Fair!

1. Sloane, S., Baillargeon, R. & Premack, D., 'Do Infants Have a Sense of Fairness?', *Psychol. Sci.* **23**, 196–204 (2012).
2. Haidt, J., 'The Emotional Dog and Its Rational Tail: A Social Intuitionist Approach to Moral Judgment', *Psychol. Rev.* **108**, 814–834 (2001).
3. Brosnan, S. F. & de Waal, F. B. M., 'Monkeys Reject Unequal Pay', *Nature* **425**, 297–299 (2003).
4. Henrich, J. et al., 'Costly Punishment Across Human Societies', *Science* **312**, 1767–1770 (2006).
5. Fehr, E. & Gächter, S., 'Altruistic Punishment in Humans', *Nature* **415**, 137–140 (2002).
6. Starmans, C., Sheskin, M. & Bloom, P., 'Why People Prefer Unequal Societies', *Nat. Hum. Behav.* **1**, 0082 (2017).
7. Rakoczy, Warneken, F. & Tomasello, M., 'The Sources of Normativity: Young Children's Awareness of the Normative Structure of Games', *Dev. Psychol.* **44**, 875 – 881 (2008).
8. Schäfer, M., Haun, D. B. M. & Tomasello, M., 'Fair Is Not Fair Everywhere', *Psychol. Sci.* **26**, 1252–1260 (2015).

9. Smith. S., 'Why People Are Rich and Poor: Republicans and Democrats Have Very Different Views', *Pew Research Center* (2017).

10. Norton, M. I. & Ariely, D., 'Building a Better America – One Wealth Quintile at a Time', *Perspect. Psychol. Sci.* **6**, 9–12 (2011).

11. Alford, J. R., Funk, C. L. & Hibbing, J. R., 'Are Political Orientations Genetically Transmitted?', *Am. Polit. Sci. Rev.* **99**, 153–167 (2005).

12. Tam, K.-P., Shu, T.-M., Ng, H. K.-S. & Tong, Y.-Y., 'Belief About Immutability of Moral Character and Punitiveness Toward Criminal Offenders', *J. Appl. Soc. Psychol.* **43**, 603–611 (2013).

13. Furnham, A., Johnson, C. & Rawles, R., 'The Determinants of Beliefs in Human Nature', *Personal. Individ. Differ.* **6**, 675–684 (1985).

14. Bastian, B. & Haslam, N., 'Immigration from the Perspective of Hosts and Immigrants: Roles of Psychological Essentialism and Social Identity', *Asian J. Soc. Psychol.* **11**, 127–140 (2008).

15. Graham, J., Haidt, J. & Nosek, B. A., 'Liberals and Conservatives Rely on Different Sets of Moral Foundations', *J. Pers. Soc. Psychol.* **96**, 1029–1046 (2009).

Chapter 2: Personal Politics

1. Bobbio, Norberto, 'Left and Right: The Significance of a Political Distinction', Wiley. Available at: http://www.wiley.com/WileyCDA/WileyTitle/productCd-0745615619.html (Accessed: 17th July 2017); Noël, A., & Thérien, J. P., *Left and Right in Global Politics* (Cambridge: Cambridge University Press, 2008).

2. Feinberg, M., Tullett, A. M., Mensch, Z., Hart, W. & Gottlieb, S., 'The Political Reference Point: How Geography Shapes Political Identity', *PLOS ONE* **12**, e0171497 (2017).

3. Lewis, G. J., 'Hans Eysenck and the First Wave of Socio-Political Genetics', *Personal. Individ. Differ.* **103**, 135–139 (2016).

4. Hatemi, P. K. et al., 'Genetic Influences on Political Ideologies: Twin Analyses of 19 Measures of Political Ideologies from Five Democracies and Genome-Wide Findings from Three Populations', *Behav. Genet.* **44**, 282–294 (2014).

5. Kanai, R., Feilden, T., Firth, C. & Rees, G., 'Political Orientations Are Correlated with Brain Structure in Young Adults', *Curr. Biol.* **21**, 677–680 (2011).

6. Méndez-Bértolo, C. et al., 'A Fast Pathway for Fear in Human Amygdala', *Nat. Neurosci.* **19**, 1041–1049 (2016).

7. Ahn, W. Y. et al., 'Nonpolitical Images Evoke Neural Predictors of Political Ideology', *Curr. Biol.* **24**, 2693–2699 (2014).

8. Schreiber, D. et al., 'Red Brain, Blue Brain: Evaluative Processes Differ in Democrats and Republicans', *PLOS ONE* **8**, e52970 (2013).

9. Oxley, D. R. et al., 'Political Attitudes Vary with Physiological Traits', *Science* **321**, 1667–1670 (2008).

10. Dodd, M. D. et al., 'The Political Left Rolls with the Good and the Political Right Confronts the Bad: Connecting Physiology and Cognition to Preferences', *Philos. Trans. R. Soc. Lond. B Biol. Sci.* **367**, 640–649 (2012).

11. Amodio, D. M., Jost, J. T., Master, S. L. & Yee, C. M., 'Neurocognitive Correlates of Liberalism and Conservatism', *Nat. Neurosci.* **10**, 1246–1247 (2007).

12. Draganski, B. et al., 'Temporal and Spatial Dynamics of Brain Structure Changes During Extensive Learning', *J. Neurosci.* **26**, 6314–6317 (2006).

13. van Leeuwen, F. & Park, J. H., 'Perceptions of Social Dangers, Moral Foundations, and Political Orientation', *Personal. Individ. Differ.* **47**, 169–173 (2009).

14. Gosling, S. D., Rentfrow, P. J. & Swann, W. B., 'A Very Brief Measure of the Big-Five Personality Domains', *J. Res. Personal.* **37**, 504–528 (2003).

15. 'Does Your Personality Influence Who You Vote For?' ScienceDaily. Available at: https://www.sciencedaily.com/releases/2008/10/081031161623.htm. (Accessed: 17th July 2017).

16. Gerber, A. S., Huber, G. A., Doherty, D., Dowling, C. M. & Ha, S. E., 'Personality and Political Attitudes: Relationships Across Issue Domains and Political Contexts', *Am. Polit. Sci. Rev.* **104**, 111–133 (2010).

17. Sylwester, K. & Purver, M., 'Twitter Language Use Reflects Psychological Differences Between Democrats and Republicans', *PLOS ONE* **10**, e0137422 (2015).

18. Samek, A. 'The Association between Personality Traits and Voting Intentions in the 2016 Presidential Election', The Evidence Base. Available at: http://evidencebase.usc.edu/?p=1158

19. Bolsen, T., 'Political Science: Partisans' Science Interests', *Nat. Hum. Behav.* **1**, s41562-017-0076-017 (2017).

20. Iyer, R., Koleva, S., Graham, J., Ditto, P. & Haidt, J., 'Understanding Libertarian Morality: The Psychological Dispositions of Self-Identified Libertarians', *PLOS ONE* **7**, e42366 (2012).

21. Sears, D. O. & Brown, C., 'Childhood and Adult Political Development', in L. Huddy, D. O. Sears & J. S. Levy (eds), *The Oxford Handbook of Political Psychology* (Oxford: Oxford University Press, 2013).

22. Funk, C. L., 'Genetic Foundations of Political Behavior', in Huddy, Sears & Levy (eds), *Oxford Handbook of Political Psychology*.

Chapter 3: Why You Always Think You're Right

1. Nisbett, R. E. & Wilson, T. D., 'Telling More Than We Can Know: Verbal Reports on Mental Processes', *Psychol. Rev.* **84**, 231–59 (1977).
2. Cohen, G. L., 'Party Over Policy: The Dominating Impact of Group Influence on Political Beliefs', *J. Pers. Soc. Psychol.* **85**, 808–822 (2003).
3. Hall, L. et al., 'How the Polls Can Be Both Spot On and Dead Wrong: Using Choice Blindness to Shift Political Attitudes and Voter Intentions', *PLOS ONE* **8**, e60554 (2013).
4. Regan, D. T. & Kilduff, M., 'Optimism About Elections: Dissonance Reduction at the Ballot Box', *Polit. Psychol.* **9**, 101–107 (1988).
5. Frenkel, O. J. & Doob, A. N., 'Post-decision Dissonance at the Polling Booth', *Can. J. Behav. Sci. Rev. Can. Sci. Comport.* **8**, 347–350 (1976).
6. Kay, A. C., Jimenez, M. C. & Jost, J. T., 'Sour Grapes, Sweet Lemons, and the Anticipatory Rationalization of the Status Quo', *Pers. Soc. Psychol. Bull.* **28**, 1300–1312 (2002).
7. Boxell, L., Gentzkow, M. & Shapiro, J. M., 'Is the Internet Causing Political Polarization? Evidence from Demographics', National Bureau of Economic Research, 2017. doi:10.3386/w23258
8. Anspach, N. M., 'The New Personal Influence: How Our Facebook Friends Influence the News We Read', *Polit. Commun.* **0**, 1–17 (2017).
9. Lord, C. G., Ross, L. & Lepper, M. R., 'Biased Assimilation and Attitude Polarization: The Effects of Prior Theories on Subsequently Considered Evidence', *J. Pers. Soc. Psychol.* **37**, 2098–2109 (1979).
10. Nickerson, R. S., 'Confirmation Bias: A Ubiquitous Phenomenon in Many Guises', *Rev. Gen. Psychol.* **2**, 175–220 (1998).

11. Kaplan, J. T., Gimbel, S. I. & Harris, S., 'Neural Correlates of Maintaining One's Political Beliefs in the Face of Counterevidence', *Sci. Rep.* **6**, 39589 (2016).

Chapter 4: What's in a Face?

1. Druckman, J. N., 'The Power of Television Images: The First Kennedy–Nixon Debate Revisited', *J. Polit.* **65**, 559–571 (2003).

2. Todorov, A., Mandisodza, A. N., Goren, A. & Hall, C. C., 'Inferences of Competence from Faces Predict Election Outcomes', *Science* **308**, 1623–1626 (2005).

3. Ballew, C. C. & Todorov, A., 'Predicting Political Elections from Rapid and Unreflective Face Judgments', *Proc. Natl. Acad. Sci.* **104**, 17948–17953 (2007).

4. Olivola, C. Y. & Todorov, A., 'Elected in 100 Milliseconds: Appearance-Based Trait Inferences and Voting', *J. Nonverbal Behav.* **34**, 83–110 (2010).

5. Little, A. C., Burriss, R. P., Jones, B. C. & Roberts, S. C., 'Facial Appearance Affects Voting Decisions', *Evol. Hum. Behav.* **28**, 18–27 (2007).

6. Sussman, A. B., Petkova, K. & Todorov, A., 'Competence Ratings in US Predict Presidential Election Outcomes in Bulgaria', *J. Exp. Soc. Psychol.* **49**, 771–775 (2013).

7. Lawson, C., Lenz, G. S., Baker, A. & Myers, M., 'Looking Like a Winner: Candidate Appearance and Electoral Success in New Democracies', *World Polit.* **62**, 561–593 (2010).

8. Na, J., Kim, S., Oh, H., Choi, I. & O'Toole, A., 'Competence Judgments Based on Facial Appearance Are Better Predictors of American Elections Than of Korean Elections', *Psychol. Sci.* **26**, 1107–1113 (2015).

9. Rule, N. O. et al., 'Polling the Face: Prediction and Consensus Across Cultures', *J. Pers. Soc. Psychol.* **98**, 1–15 (2010).

10. Antonakis, J. & Dalgas, O., 'Predicting Elections: Child's Play!', *Science* **323**, 1183–1183 (2009).

11. Verhulst, B., Lodge, M. & Lavine, H., 'The Attractiveness Halo: Why Some Candidates are Perceived More Favorably than Others', *J. Nonverbal Behav.* **34**, 111–117 (2010).

12. Berggren, N., Jordahl, H. & Poutvaara, P., 'The Looks of a Winner: Beauty and Electoral Success', *J. Public Econ.* **94**, 8–15 (2010).

13. Gheorghiu, A. I., Callan, M. J. & Skylark, W. J., 'Facial Appearance Affects Science Communication', *Proc. Natl. Acad. Sci. U. S. A.* **114**, 5970–5975 (2017).

14. Rule, N. O. & Ambady, N., 'Democrats and Republicans Can Be Differentiated from Their Faces', *PLOS ONE* **5**, e8733 (2010).

15. Olivola, C. Y., Sussman, A. B., Tsetsos, K., Kang, O. E. & Todorov, A., 'Republicans Prefer Republican-Looking Leaders: Political Facial Stereotypes Predict Candidate Electoral Success Among Right-Leaning Voters', *Soc. Psychol. Personal. Sci.* **3**, 605–613 (2012).

Chapter 5: Making the Headlines

1. Iyengar, S., Peters, M. D. & Kinder, D. R., 'Experimental Demonstrations of the "Not-So-Minimal" Consequences of Television News Programs', *Am. Polit. Sci. Rev.* **76**, 848–858 (1982).

2. Knight, B. G. & Chiang, C.-F., 'Media Bias and Influence: Evidence from Newspaper Endorsements', National Bureau of Economic Research, 2008. doi:10.3386/w14445

3. Cohen, B. C., *The Press and Foreign Policy* (Institute of Governmental Studies, University of California, 1963).

4. Iyengar, Peters, Kinder, 'Experimental Demonstrations'.

5. Tversky, A. & Kahneman, D., 'Availability: A Heuristic for Judging Frequency and Probability', *Cognit. Psychol.* **5**, 207–232 (1973).

6. Haddock, G., 'It's Easy to Like or Dislike Tony Blair: Accessibility Experiences and the Favourability of Attitude Judgments', *Br. J. Psychol. Lond. Engl. 1953* **93**, 257–267 (2002).

7. Petrocik, J. R., 'Issue Ownership in Presidential Elections, with a 1980 Case Study', *Am. J. Polit. Sci.* **40,** 825–850 (1996); Petrocik, J. R., Benoit, W. L. & Hansen, G. J., 'Issue Ownership and Presidential Campaigning, 1952–2000', *Polit. Sci. Q.* **118**, 599–626 (2003).

8. Zajonc, R., 'Attitudinal Effects of Mere Exposure', *J. Pers. Soc. Psychol.* **9**, 1–27 (1968).

9. Bornstein, R. F., 'Exposure and Affect: Overview and Meta-Analysis of Research 1968–1987', *Psychol. Bull.* **106**, 265–89 (1989).

10. Hasher, L., Goldstein, D. & Toppino, T., 'Frequency and the Conference of Referential Validity'. *J. Verbal Learn. Verbal Behav.* **16**, 107–112 (1977).

11. Tversky, A. & Kahneman, D., 'The Framing of Decisions and the Psychology of Choice', *Science* **211**, 453–458 (1981).

12. Nelson, T. E., Clawson, R. A. & Oxley, Z. M., 'Media Framing of a Civil Liberties Conflict and Its Effect on Tolerance', *Am. Polit. Sci. Rev.* **91**, 567–583 (1997).

Chapter 6: Faking It

1. Fessler, D. M. T., Pisor, A. C. & Holbrook, C., 'Political Orientation Predicts Credulity Regarding Putative Hazards', *Psychol. Sci.* **28**, 651–660 (2017).

2. Reinhart, C. M. & Rogoff, K. S., 'Growth in a Time of Debt', National Bureau of Economic Research, 2010. doi:10.3386/w15639

3. Herndon, T., Ash, M. & Pollin, R., 'Does High Public Debt Consistently Stifle Economic Growth? A Critique of Reinhart and Rogoff', *Camb. J. Econ.* **38**, 257–279 (2014).

4. Carter, T. J., Ferguson, M. J. & Hassin, R. R., 'A Single Exposure to the American Flag Shifts Support Toward Republicanism Up to 8 Months Later', *Psychol. Sci.* **22**, 1011–1018 (2011).

5. Klein, R. A. et al., 'Investigating Variation in Replicability', *Soc. Psychol.* **45**, 142–152 (2014).

6. Sumner, P. et al., 'The Association Between Exaggeration in Health-Related Science News and Academic Press Releases: Retrospective Observational Study. *BMJ* **349**, g7015 (2014).

7. Flaherty, D. K., 'The Vaccine–Autism Connection: A Public Health Crisis Caused by Unethical Medical Practices and Fraudulent Science', *Ann. Pharmacother.* **45**, 1302–1304 (2011).

8. Kull, S., Ramsay, C. & Lewis, E., 'Misperceptions, the Media, and the Iraq War', *Polit. Sci. Q.* **118**, 569–598 (2003).

9. Hart, P. S. & Nisbet, E. C., 'Boomerang Effects in Science Communication: How Motivated Reasoning and Identity Cues Amplify Opinion Polarization About Climate Mitigation Policies', *Commun. Res.* **39**, 701–723 (2012).

10. Leviston, Z., Walker, I. & Morwinski, S., 'Your Opinion on Climate Change Might Not Be As Common As You Think', *Nat. Clim. Change* **3**, 334 (2013).

11. van der Linden, S., Leiserowitz, A., Rosenthal, S. & Maibach, E., 'Inoculating the Public Against Misinformation About Climate Change', *Glob. Chall.* **1**, n/a-n/a (2017).

Chapter 7: Are You Being Nudged?

1. Youyou, W., Kosinski, M. & Stillwell, D., 'Computer-Based Personality Judgments Are More Accurate Than Those Made By Humans', *Proc. Natl. Acad. Sci.* **112**, 1036–1040 (2015).

2. Broockman, D. & Kalla, J., 'Durably Reducing Transphobia: A Field Experiment on Door-to-Door Canvassing', *Science* **352**, 220–224 (2016).

3. Bond, R. M. et al., 'A 61-Million-Person Experiment In Social Influence and Political Mobilization', *Nature* **489**, 295–298 (2012).

4. Gerber, A. S., Green, D. P. & Larimer, C. W., 'Social Pressure and Voter Turnout: Evidence from a Large-Scale Field Experiment', *Am. Polit. Sci. Rev.* **102**, 33–48 (2008).

5. John, P., MacDonald, E. & Sanders, M., 'Targeting Voter Registration with Incentives: A Randomized Controlled Trial of a Lottery in a London Borough', *Elect. Stud.* **40**, 170–175 (2015).

6. Gerber, A. S. & Green, D. P., 'The Effects of Canvassing, Telephone Calls, and Direct Mail on Voter Turnout: A Field Experiment', *Am. Polit. Sci. Rev.* **94**, 653–663 (2000).

Chapter 8: A Silent Majority

1. Grönlund, K. & Milner, H., 'The Determinants of Political Knowledge in Comparative Perspective', *Scand. Polit. Stud.* **29**, 386–406 (2006).

2. Prior, M., 'News vs. Entertainment: How Increasing Media Choice Widens Gaps in Political Knowledge and Turnout', *Am. J. Polit. Sci.* **49**, 577–592 (2005).

3. Crompton, T., 'Perceptions Matter: The Common Cause UK Values Survey', Common Cause Foundation, 2016.

4. Spector, P. E., 'Perceived Control by Employees: A Meta-Analysis of Studies Concerning Autonomy and Participation at Work', *Hum. Relat.* **39**, 1005–1016 (1986).

5. Skinner, E. A., Wellborn, J. G. & Connell, J. P., 'What It Takes to Do Well in School and Whether I've Got It: The Role of Perceived Control in Children's Engagement and School Achievement', *J. Educ. Psychol.* 22–32 (1990).

6. Karsh, N. & Eitam, B., 'I Control Therefore I Do: Judgments of Agency Influence Action Selection', *Cognition* **138**, 122–131 (2015).

7. Denver, D., Hands, G. & MacAllister, I., 'Constituency Marginality and Turnout in Britain Revisited', *Br. Elections Parties Rev.* **13**, 174–194 (2003).

8. Karp, J. A. & Banducci, S. A., 'Political Efficacy and Participation in Twenty-Seven Democracies: How Electoral Systems Shape Political Behaviour', *Br. J. Polit. Sci.* **38**, 311–334 (2008).

9. Schoen, H. & Schumann, S., 'Personality Traits, Partisan Attitudes, and Voting Behavior. Evidence from Germany', *Polit. Psychol.* **28**, 471–498 (2007).

10. Marien, S., Hooghe, M. & Quintelier, E., 'Inequalities in Non-institutionalised Forms of Political Participation: A Multi-level Analysis of 25 Countries', *Polit. Stud.* **58**, 187–213 (2010).

Conclusion: Democracy for Humans

1. Lau, R. R. & Redlawsk, D. P., 'Voting Correctly', *Am. Polit. Sci. Rev.* **91**, 585–598 (1997).

2. Duarte, J. L. et al., 'Political Diversity Will Improve Social Psychological Science', *Behav. Brain Sci.* **38**, e130 (2015).

3. Lachman, M. E. & Weaver, S. L., 'The Sense of Control as a Moderator of Social Class Differences in Health and Well-being', *J. Pers. Soc. Psychol.* **74**, 763–773 (1998)

4. Our World In Data. Available at: https://ourworldindata.org/. (Accessed: 17th July 2017)

ACKNOWLEDGEMENTS

My first major lesson in the psychology of politics was in my late teens, when I spent a lot of time arguing with my mum about the war in Iraq. In the run up to the US/UK invasion, she chaired the local Stop the War coalition. At the time I felt convinced we had a duty to remove Saddam Hussein and that the US/UK would take full responsibility for reconstructing Iraq after the war. After the invasion it became increasingly clear that I was wrong. I'm sorry to my mum for being such an argumentative teenager at the time, but I'm extremely grateful for her continued passion and engagement in politics.

Realising I was wrong about something so important (especially having been so convinced at the time) has shaped my interest ever since, not just in politics, but also in the reasons behind our political beliefs and why we sometimes hold them so single-mindedly.

As an undergraduate, my studies at the University of Bristol started to give me some insight into this. I owe a lot to the many excellent lecturers there, who spent so much time discussing ideas with me, inspiring me to go on to study psychology. I'd like to pay particular tribute to Nick Scott-Samuel and the now-late Tom Trościanko and Richard Gregory, who collectively inspired me to study for a PhD to understand the psychology of how we see the world.

I'd like to thank the University of Bristol again for making me an Honorary Senior Research Fellow in 2015, and pay particular thanks to Policy Bristol (and Kat Walls) for helping me to set up the Bristol Politics Cafe in the run up to the 2015 election. Many of the ideas for this book started to take form in the lectures and debates of those sessions. In discussing how academic research might contribute to broader political issues, I started to realise that many people were looking for different ways to approach political issues, from a more considered and reflective perspective. I hope the open, informed and earnest tone of those 'politics cafes' is reflected in this book.

I regret that I didn't learn more about the psychology of politics as an undergraduate. So I'd like to particularly thank Chris Donlan at University College London, and Kate Plaisted-Grant and Jason Rentfrow at the University of Cambridge for giving me the chance to develop lectures on this topic, the content of which has largely formed the backbone of this book. The lectures seem to have received very positive student feedback; I hope this book proves to be equally well received.

I also owe an enormous debt to many colleagues with whom I've discussed the psychology of politics over the last few years. Particular thanks to Gary Lewis (who also very kindly reviewed an early draft of the book), Carmen Lefevre, Colin Davis, Jeff Bowers, Steve Lewandowsky, Nathalia Gjersoe, Alan Renwick, Peter John, Ric Bailey, Nicholas Wright, Jens Madsen, Clare Bissell, Caitlin Mullin and Annelien Buedts.

I'd also like to thank the many fantastic students I've had the honour to teach or supervise over the last few years. Nothing inspires me to think and learn more than the opportunity to share that knowledge. I'd especially like to thank James Glenister, who also read an earlier draft of the book.

I'm also lucky to have met Ed Sapira and be a member of his tech-politics club Newspeak House in Bethnal Green, London. The psychology of politics and the role of technology in politics are tightly intertwined, and I've had some of the most interesting conversations about politics and psychology over the last year at Newspeak, which also helped to shape and inform this book.

Finally I'd like to thank my publishers Elliott and Thompson, and in particular Pippa Crane and Jennie Condell. From the first moment we met, I was really excited that we could do something quite special with this book at such a poignant time. I've heard so many horror stories from colleagues who have worked with publishers who have pushed them to oversell research or taken a factory line approach to book writing. They've been the exact opposite. To be honest, if you enjoy reading this book, it will largely be thanks to Pippa and Jennie, who have worked so hard in helping me to find a way to communicate the science of why we vote the way we do.

INDEX